Redefining Mr. Right

A Career Woman's Guide to Choosing a Mate

JANET Z. GILER, M.F.C.C.
KATHLEEN NEUMEYER

NEW HARBINGER PUBLICATIONS, INC.
MARIN PUBLICATIONS

Publisher's Note

This publication is designed to provide accurate and authoritative information in regard to the subject matter covered. It is sold with the understanding that neither the publisher nor the authors is engaged in rendering chiropractic, legal, medical or psychiatric services. If expert assistance or counseling is needed, the services of a competent professional should be sought.

Library of Congress Catalog Card Number: 92-081724
ISBN 1-879237-30-X Paperback
ISBM 1-879237-31-8 Hardcover

Published by
New Harbinger Publications & Marin Publications
5674 Shattuck Avenue
Oakland CA 94609

Printed in the United States of America

Cover by
SHELBY DESIGNS AND ILLUSTRATES

Cover Photograph by
Kirk Johnson

Edited by
Nina Sonenberg & Richard Gosse

Typesetting by
Daniel Bender

To my aunt, Dinah Mellon, in recognition of all she taught me about relationships, and to my husband Karl and my son Conrad, for without their love, support and willingness to work things out, I wouldn't have the experience to know how relationships work.

-JZG

To Andy and Kari, beloved anchors.

-KN

Acknowledgments

Many thanks to all the women and men who shared their love stories with us; to Janet Z. Giler's clients, students, and friends; to Richard Gosse of Marin Publications; to Judith Stevens-Long for moral support; to Karl Metzenberg, David Savion, and Roberta Wax for assistance with the preparation of the manuscript; to Ann Russo for research; and to Andrew Neumeyer for preparing the charts and graphs.

Table of Contents

Chapter Four cont:

Chapter Five:
Conflicts of the Career Woman: The Yes, But Game 85

Chapter Six:
Sexual Issues: The Myth of
Fleeing Men & Suffocating Women 103

Chapter Seven:
Grown-Up Love for the Nineties 115

Introduction

I know my mind and I have made my choice;
...Love me or love me not, you have no voice.

-Edna St. Vincent Millay
(1892-1950)

*E*veryone wants to be in love.

In the United States today, there are nearly 70 million singles—more than ever before in history. Some of them are already in love, but most are still looking for someone special. Their search has spawned a whole singles industry—singles dances, singles magazines and newspapers, video dating and matchmaking services. Singles mingle at singles bars, frequent trendy gyms, and advertise themselves in the classified sections of newspapers and magazines. They crowd into seminars trying to find the right place to meet Mr. or Ms. Right. Few of them want to hear that it isn't *where* you are...but *how* you are within yourself that determines whether or not you meet the right man. Moreover, it's not enough just to meet him. You have to know him when you see him.

Chances are, you've been looking for the wrong guy. Most women were brought up to believe that the ideal mate is a man who is a few years older, will earn more money, and be a good provider. We strive to marry older, richer, taller, and smarter than we are.

But the truth is that the right man for a 1990s woman is a far different fellow than the man who was right for women who came before us, because they were living very different lives. A woman who expects to remain in the work force all of her life, continuing to give her career a high priority alongside her relationships and her family, needs a man who can meet some of the same kinds of emotional needs for her that her mother met for her father. She needs a man who understands the stresses of her job, who can share in household and child care responsibilities, and who is not threatened by her success or by her ability to earn as much or more than he does.

If a woman is extremely intelligent and well-educated, she is not likely to meet many men who are smarter and more educated than she. The more money she earns, the smaller the pool of men who are capable of earning more. But after all, if she can provide well for herself, she doesn't really need a man who earns more than she does.

If a woman married in her late teens or early twenties, as almost all women in previous generations did, it made sense to marry a man a few years older, who was mature, ready to settle down, and capable of working to earn a living. But if a woman is marrying in her thirties or forties, what logical reason is there for choosing an older man? The older one gets, the less important age range is in human relationships. Five years is a long time between 13 and 18, or between 19 and 24, but the relative maturity level and arena of shared experience between 47 and 52 are quite similar. A man of 47 is as appropriate a mate for a 52-year-old woman as he is for a 42-year-old woman. The fact that women live longer than men, on the average, is another reason why marrying a younger man may be a good choice.

A woman who has delayed marriage into her thirties or beyond, and a woman who has been married before, may need to reconsider whether or not it is important to marry older, richer, taller, and smarter. She may need to be open to the possibility of marrying a man who is five to ten years younger than she is; more than five years older than she is; or a man who earns about the same or even less than she does; or who is less educated than she is.

Almost every woman likes to think that her man is smarter than she is, but there is a variety of kinds of intelligence—linguistic, logistical, spatial, artistic, kinesthetic, as well as the more formal sort of intelligence measured on Stanford-Binet Intelligence Quotient tests. There is also common sense, shrewdness, intuition, the ability to understand other people, and "street smarts." Interestingly, most women seem to be able to find ways in which the man they love is superior to them. A more accurate description is that he is smarter than she is in some areas and she may be smarter in others. A woman who has a Ph.D. in English literature and is married to a construction crew foreman with a high school education says that he is really much more clever than she is, and knows much more about fixing things than she does. A female physicist married to an advertising copywriter says that he is really much more verbal than she is, and much more intellectual. Even women who concede that they are smarter than their mates insist that he is more practical, or more down-to-earth. None of these women believes that she "settled" when she chose the man she did. Each thinks he is wonderful.

The notion of "marrying up" involves finding "a good catch." But most women would agree that their goal is to find the right mate for a love that will last a lifetime. For her book, *Married People; Staying Together in the Age of Divorce*, Francine Klagsbrun interviewed couples who had long and happy marriages. The common factors she found among contented couples were an ability to change and to tolerate change, an ability to accept the unchangeable, trust, a balance of dependencies, an enjoyment of one another, an assumption of permanence, and luck. None of the wives said the reason that she was happy was because her husband was a professional man or because he was six-foot-two and still had all his hair. Who was smarter or who was taller seemed to have nothing to do with lifelong contentment.

Women who have not yet found the right man need to redefine what they are looking for. Mr. Right is a man who shares your values and is as ready for a relationship as you are. It is good if the two of you enjoy some of the same pastimes, but it is not necessary for you to have identical interests. If you share a fondness for sailing and you both love to eat in restaurants, you can do those things together. If he likes to play golf and you like to play tennis, you can each pursue your own sport with other friends.

Relationships usually work out best when the couple shares the same values and some complementary personal traits. Being with someone who is just like you gets boring; being with someone who is completely your opposite, while attractive to begin with, can be stressful over the long haul.

Dr. Joyce Brothers, in her 1984 book, *What Every Woman Ought to Know About Love*, cites a Columbia University Intimacy Formula indicating there are five factors involved in determining how long it takes to meet a mate:

1. How much opportunity you create
2. How selective you are
3. How much initiative you take
4. How desirable you are to the men who like you
5. How skilled you are at sustaining a relationship

All five of these factors are within your control. The odds, quite frankly, are against Prince Charming riding up to your condo on a white steed while you are inside watching the soaps and eating a microwaved dinner. The prince--or a reasonable facsimile--*is* out there, but you have to get out there and look for him. You need to create as much opportunity as possible for him to find you; to take the initiative when necessary, and to be open to a relationship when it happens.

Being Ready

Not everyone is ready to begin and continue a relationship with a prospective spouse. Just being single isn't enough. If you have unfinished business-hurt, anger, or betrayed feelings-left over from a divorce or a broken relationship, these can get in the way of your meeting the right mate. You may be too leery of getting hurt again, or too distrustful, or just too angry to give the person you are meeting a fair chance. Frequently women who have gone through a traumatic divorce, or who have been abused either during childhood or as adults, suffer from low self-esteem which prevents them from connecting with men. No amount of flirting or learning the right ice-breakers can compensate for low self-esteem. If you don't like who you are, nobody else can make up for the love and attention you aren't giving yourself.

Exercise:

Make a list of the good qualities about yourself. On one side of the page, list positive qualities about the way you *are*. Some examples would be, "I am smart, I am pretty, I am kind, I am considerate, I have a good sense of humor."

On the other side of the sheet, make a list of positive things you *do*. Examples would be, "I can ice-skate very well, I am a good amateur photographer, I make killer linguine, and I am a very good bookkeeper."

If you can't come up with at least ten good things about yourself, your self-esteem needs a jump-start. You might consider finding a good therapist and getting some professional help in feeling better about yourself. You have to love yourself first, before someone else will.

Being Reasonable

Part of finding the right mate is a numbers game. As the fairy tale taught us, you have to kiss a lot of frogs before you meet the handsome prince. How many suitors you have to audition before you find the right one depends on how selective you are. A reasonably selective adult will like approximately 20 percent of the people he or she meets. If you like less than 20 out of 100, you are highly selective. If you like more than 20, you're fairly easy to please. Most women will have to meet between 100 to 200 available men before they find someone compatible. Very selective women may need to meet 800, while those who are easy to please might find Prince Charming in the first batch of 100 men. You simply cannot meet enough people by sitting home waiting for your friends to introduce you. You need to seize the initiative and start planning a strategy by which you can increase the number of potential mates you meet.

CHAPTER ONE

Looking for Love in
All the Wrong Decades

Everyone has heard the saying, "Be careful what you wish for because it might come true." It suggests all you have to do is decide what you want and go after it. But knowing what you want is not that simple to figure out. Without realizing it, many women are looking in the 1990s for the man Mother found in the 1940s and 1950s. Mother grew up during the depression or pre-World War II, and married in an era when a woman stayed home, did volunteer work for the PTA and the church, was a Cub Scout den mother, and drove car pools in her Woody. Dad's job was to earn the living, and his paycheck was sufficient to support the family. Mother had dinner on the table when Dad came home at night, and she felt that he was being very helpful if he pitched in to dry while she washed the dishes. His major household chores were to keep the grass mowed on Saturdays, the car lubricated, and the household appliances in good repair. The house and the kids were women's work, and a man whose wife had to work wasn't much of a man. A good husband was a good provider.

For the 1990s career woman who owns her own car, her own condominium, and her own Individual Retirement Account, to be looking for a man just like Dear Old Dad makes about as much sense as for her to be out shopping for the Frigidaire that Betty Furness hawked in the television commercials of the 1950s. If you aren't going to live a "Leave It To Beaver" lifestyle, it's a waste of time to look for Ward Cleaver.

Marrying Her Mother's Ideal Son-in-Law

Beth's parents married when her mother was 19 and just out of high school and her father was a 21-year-old career Air Force officer. Beth was born a year later, and her mother stayed home to raise her and her younger siblings.

"She never went to college and she never worked. That was the expected role in the 1950s," Beth says.

"To her credit, she was a wonderful mother and she encouraged me to further my education. I was a good student, but when I decided to go on to Harvard Medical School, my parents were reluctant. I had been a nursing major, and that pleased them. They thought that nursing was an appropriate career choice for a woman. When I wanted to be a doctor, they were taken aback. They worried that I had chosen a lifestyle that was going to be too hard for me. I was a first child, and in some ways, even though I wanted to do something different, a part of me still tried very hard to please my folks and do what women do. I think that it is not unusual in my generation for women to strike out professionally, but still have some residual emotional ties to the traditional roles," Beth said.

Beth finished her undergraduate degree early and spent a few months working before beginning medical school. During that time, she met a handsome first year medical student at the state university.

"He was a year older than I, from a very good family, well-dressed and well-educated, the kind of man any mother would love to have as a son-in-law. I fell in love with him, but I think now that he was not a good choice for me," she said.

Beth and Bob carried on a long distance romance during her first year at Harvard Medical School and were married the next summer in the rural Southern town where she grew up. Although she was at the top of her Harvard class, Beth transferred to the state university, like a dutiful wife, to be near Bob.

The marriage lasted only a year and a half.

"He was very traditional in his outlook on life. He was from the South, so he had the same background I did, and it was difficult for him to have a wife as powerful as I was. I graduated number two in my class," she said.

The breakup of the marriage devastated Beth, who was accustomed to succeeding in everything she did. She finished medical school and completed residencies in general surgery and plastic surgery.

Nine years after her divorce was final, she met Larry, an advertising copywriter. They dated for three years before marrying, when both of them were 35.

"Larry is entirely different from Bob. By the time I met him, I was already a doctor, and a plastic surgeon. He knew what he was getting into. It was a second marriage for him too, and both of us were already formed, so to speak. We had our eyes more wide open than the first time."

Beth said one of the things that attracted her to Larry was that his job was so different from hers.

"In the same field there is always the element of competition," she said. "It is more interesting to be with someone who does something entirely different. It gives me a window into another world," she says.

Beth admits that she chose her first husband because he was a man of whom her parents would approve. Because she believed that she was disappointing her family with her untraditional career choice, she felt impelled to redeem herself by marrying well by their standards. Her idea of the appropriate suitor was the one her mother would have chosen for her—an attractive young man who was slightly older, from a "good" family with similar values, who was clearly upwardly mobile and would be able to provide well for her—even though her own career choice meant she would never need a good provider.

Choosing that kind of a man brought with it the attendant problems that his expectations were to have a traditional marriage with a wife who was less accomplished than he was, who would nurture him in the way Beth's mother had nurtured her husband.

An older, more mature Beth chose for her second husband a man who respected her for her accomplishments, and who understood how important her profession was to her and to the way she lived her life. When Larry met and fell in love with Beth, she had a separate identity of her own—she was a doctor, a plastic surgeon. As Beth put it, "He knew what he was getting into."

Phase I and Phase II Relationships

Because women grow up identifying with Mother, they tend to internalize her values. In many cases, young women have incorporated a totally distorted image of what married love is supposed to be, based on their own notion of their parents' marriage, with a romanticized overlay of images from movies, popular music, books, and poetry about what love is. Their images are often highly romantic, based on the unrealistic medieval concept of courtly love, of a knight riding up on a white charger to rescue the fair damsel in the tower. The 1990s version of Prince Charming, after all, is actor Richard Gere, a handsome, older, rich man, popping up through the sun-roof of a sleek limousine, his arms filled with roses for Julia Roberts, in the film "Pretty Woman." We still dream of the White Knight.

Often in relationships formed in early adulthood, a woman is seeking her other half, acting out her fantasies of completion. She expects the man to be her soul mate. Together they will be whole. When a woman marries right out of high school or college, before she has formulated an identity for herself based on her own achievements, she is likely to use these unconscious criteria in making her choice.   Unfortunately, these Phase I relationships do not always lend themselves to the day-in-and-day-out exigencies of life.   Some end in divorce. The ones that endure usually do so because the partners have been able to transform the relationship into a more mature and realistic relationship built on interdependency and greater autonomy.

Women who remain unmarried during their twenties, or for a significant period while they are building their own identity through work or life experiences, should be ready to move directly into a Phase II relationship.   In Phase II relationships, the couples are older, have lived more of their lives alone, have recovered from some Phase I relationship in which they were trying to live out a completion fantasy, and are ready to be more autonomous and interrelated.   These relationships are characterized by respect, mutual negotiations, and give-and-take.   For some couples, these relationships come with more encumbrances; there may be children from one or both previous marriages; there may be old entanglements with other people which need to be sorted out. The love that endures in these marriages may involve less fantasy, but the relationships are characterized by a feeling of partnership.

It is important to think about where you are in terms of your own identity formation because what you need in a lover or spouse is different depending on your stage of life. There is no formula for the ideal mate. A man who is perfect for one woman is not perfect for another, and a man who might have seemed perfect for you in your twenties will not necessarily seem perfect in your forties. At different stages of your life, your needs are different. We all have different ideas about what love is. Although most people agree that they believe that the person they love should be both a lover and a friend, they run into trouble when they start dredging up their fantasies about what love is. In some cases, images emerge about status symbols, sex objects, and notions that rely heavily on projecting an unfinished and in many cases unconscious notion of self upon the other. Among younger people, the fantasy frequently revolves around a primary myth of fusion and complementarity—that the two people coming together can and will become a whole person.   These relationships look very different from the ones described by women and men who are looking the second time around, or women and men who have delayed marriage while investing in a career.

For mature women who are secure in their own identities, finding someone who is going to help them define themselves isn't the issue; they want partners to share their lives with, whether that means raising children, or sharing in the successes and failures of their careers, or living as companions into the golden years of retirement. These women have a very different picture about what Mr. Right looks like.

Many of the career women we interviewed for this book had recognized the need to set aside the romanticized notion of love in which one person was expected to be part of their internalized fantasy, a religious experience, and their better half all rolled into one. Maybe it was life experience which got them this far, or maybe it was the experience of living through many disappointments when a fantasy lover gave way to a real person who belched, needed the extra skosh' in his pants, or had begun to lose his hair.

Women who have successfully made the transition into Phase II relationships have not given up the expectation of having romance in their lives. Love and marriage include romance, as well as romantic moments, but a mature relationship involves a real man and a real woman, and not knights in shining armor or ladies in glass slippers.

The Changing American Family

There are more single people in the United States now than ever before in history. Nearly half of all marriages end in divorce, and lumping together those who have been divorced with those who have never been married, there are nearly 70 million Americans over 18 who show up on the census as single adults.

Even though a high percentage of Americans are single, somehow we still think that it is "normal" to be married and part of a traditional family. The concept of what is traditional or even normal in terms of family life is determined by what we knew growing up. People raised in the 1950s by parents who grew up before World War II tend to view their parents' generation as normal. However, many demographers actually refer to that generation as non-normative because a pattern of delayed marriages, delayed child-bearing, and decreased family size has been the trend since the late 1890s, with the exception of the 1940s and 1950s, when people married earlier and had more children.

The change in the American family was caused by a combination of sociological, economic, and structural elements. Before the Industrial Revolution, work and family roles were tied together. Husbands and wives worked together on a farm or in a family business. The segregation of work and family roles is a post-industrial phenomenon. What we call traditional family roles have only been traditional during the second half of this century. The inherent bipolar complementarity of sex roles, where men go to work and women stay home, is a phenomenon quite new to our history, since the 1950s. The agrarian family was actually a more symmetrical arrangement.

Women began to work outside the home in the 1880s, generally in mill town factories before they married. During World War II, when women were needed in the labor force because most able-bodied men were overseas, no one considered it unfeminine to help the country. It was not only patriotic but quite socially acceptable to work in factories as part of the war effort. Economic necessity dictated what was socially acceptable. Rather than being preordained phenomena, roles and our conception of them change according to economic need. Social thought follows suit—with some lag time in which we attempt to absorb the changes.

The Industrial Revolution moved extended families out of the countryside and into the city. The breakdown of the American family began with this shift from an agrarian economy. Not only were families smaller, with less reliance on and cohabitation with extended kin, but the partnership of work and family roles that had been shared by children and parents and by husband and wife, was unraveled. Whereas the agrarian family's roles were highly enmeshed and interdependent, in the industrial economy which replaced it, work and family roles began to be seen as oppositional and separate. Women and children were only integrated into the work force as the need arose.

The 1990s economic climate is far different from the 1950s. Wages were high in the postwar economic boom, making it possible for one person to support a family. This allowed the segregation of roles; it became economically feasible for the husband to be the provider and the wife to be the full-time nurturer. If the economics were still the same, this role segregation might still exist. However, in the 1990s, most families cannot get along on a single income. It is no longer a matter of privilege for women to work; women must work to help support their families.

The Women's Movement, which began in the 1960s, espoused the notion that women had a right to fulfill themselves through work, and promoted equality for women in the work place. Although many of these ideas have taken hold in the popular culture, and some progress has been made for women, as a society we have still not completely accepted the idea of women in the work place. Despite the fact that 60 percent of all mothers work, our collective fantasy has not changed much from the "Leave it to Beaver" and "Ozzie and Harriet" model of how family life should be. One of the most watched television shows of the 1980s featured Bill Cosby playing a gynecologist and his television wife a lawyer, but we never saw her actually working. However, a successful sit-com of the early 1990s, "Roseanne," shows a middle class housewife dealing with the house and children while working at menial jobs to help make ends meet, in a fairly egalitarian relationship with her blue collar spouse.

Many women do still work in what Susan Faludi, in her 1992 book *Backlash*, terms "low-paid female ghettos." America's secretarial pool is 99.2 percent female. On the other hand, the U.S. Bureau of Labor Statistics reports that the percentage of women executives, administrators, and managers among all the managers in the American work force has risen from 32.4 percent in 1983 to 41 percent in 1991.

Initially the idea of women working was viewed as heresy; a good man's wife didn't work. For men, having a working wife was an ideological blow to their identity and feelings of competence. It meant failing to perform their role as provider. The exception to this conception of roles is directly related to economic need; in immigrant families women have always worked until achieving middle class status, when they retired. The current economic reality, combined with sociological predictions that women will live a longer portion of their lives single and as heads of households than at any other time in history, indicates that women are going to continue to be heavily represented in the labor force.

Before the turn of the century, the average woman bore her last child when she was 33. She was 56 by the time that child married, and after that, she had only another 10 to 15 years to live. The average American woman in her early thirties in the 1990s will spend a larger part of her life single than her mother's generation, due to divorce and delayed marriages. She will spend a smaller percentage of her life as a wife, and will have 10 to 15 years more non-parenting time than her mother expected to have 40 years ago. In 1920, the average woman lived to be 55. Today she can expect to live to almost 80.

Although today's women spend less time engaged in child-rearing than the generations that preceded them, our perceptions of sex roles have not changed nearly as much as the actual roles have. Women spend a greater portion of their lives in roles other than that of wife and mother, which historically has been one of the most dominant factors in their identities.

These changes are significant because they influence what women want, what roles they wish to play, and how they see themselves in relationship to men.

Changing Needs

Women's needs in a mate have changed dramatically over the years. In 1906, when Jessie married Grover in Greensburg, Indiana, she was marrying a young man she'd known all through elementary and high school. They had grown up together in the same community, attended the same church, and had the same friends. They set up housekeeping near their own parents and grandparents, in a setting where each of them had a lot of support in a variety of relationships. They knew their neighbors; they knew the merchants and the banker. Grover joined his father-in-law in his grain business, and farmed along with his own father and uncles. When children were born, the grandmothers and the aunts were there to help. In fact, it was not unusual for several generations of a family to live together in the same household.

With so many other relatives and friends as part of their support group, Jessie and Grover did not have to rely on each other to meet all of their emotional needs. At the same time, their lives were so intertwined with so many other people, that separating would have been difficult. Perhaps it is not so surprising that Jessie's marriage—like the majority of those of her day—lasted through more than 50 years, six children, and 19 grandchildren.

During the early part of the century, few couples divorced. Marriage was forever, and divorce was a scandal. Today, we expect our mates to be everything to us forever—a lover, a friend, a parent, a companion, a sex object, and a support system. At the same time, we have much more permission to break off the relationship if it doesn't live up to all of our expectations. We want more, but we don't know how to get it or how to keep it, and when the going gets rough, we discard it and start over. The trend is toward greater expectations in what we are looking for in a relationship, coupled with greater societal permission to terminate relationships, which leaves relationships less stable. The task of finding a mate and maintaining a relationship which will remain satisfying over the course of a lifetime has become more challenging than ever.

The Man Shortage Myth

On June 2, 1986, *Newsweek* magazine ran a cover story trumpeting the supposed findings of an academic study proving that a 40-year-old single woman had a greater chance of being killed by a terrorist than of getting married.

"The traumatic news," Newsweek said, "came buried in an arid demographic study titled, innocently enough, 'Marriage Patterns in the United States.' According to the report, white, college-educated women born in the mid-50s who are still single at 30 have only a 20 percent chance of marrying. By the age of 35, the odds drop to 5 percent. Forty-year-olds are more likely to be killed by a terrorist: they have a minuscule 2.6 probability of tying the knot."

Women were panicking, the magazine reported.

A New York therapist, Bonnie Maslin, was quoted as saying, "One patient told me, 'I feel like my mother's finger is wagging at me, telling me I shouldn't have waited.'"

A 36-year-old woman told the *Wall Street Journal* that being single didn't bother her at all until she heard those statistics. After that, she felt depressed. A 35-year-old woman was quoted in USA Today as saying, "I hadn't even thought about getting married until I read those horror stories." Therapists told the *Los Angeles Times* that single women were "obsessed" with marriage.

The story that traumatized millions of American women began accidentally. A reporter for the Stamford (Connecticut) *Advocate* was assigned to write a feature called, "Romance: Is It In Or Out?" for the Valentine's Day edition of the newspaper. The reporter, Lisa Marie Petersen, went out to the Stamford Town Center Mall and interviewed a few men who were shopping for chocolates and funny Valentine cards, then decided to telephone the sociology department at Yale University to get some background information or statistics to give her story some substance.

Her call was referred to Neil Bennett, a sociologist who had just completed an unpublished study on women's marriage patterns, along with Harvard economist David Bloom and Yale graduate student Patricia Craig. Bennett told Petersen that he had the results of an unpublished report showing that college educated women who had never been married had a 20 percent chance of finding a husband by the time they were 30, a 5 percent chance by the time they were 35, and that the odds dropped to only a 1.3 percent chance by the time they were 40.

Petersen, who was 27 and unmarried at the time, found the statistics shocking, but she never doubted that they were accurate. "We usually just take anything from good schools. If it's a study from Yale, we just put it in the paper," she told Susan Faludi.

After the *Advocate* ran Petersen's front page story, it was picked up by the Associated Press and by newspapers around the world, creating a media frenzy. The statistics were discussed on television sit-coms, including "Designing Women" and "Kate and Allie," and in such feature films as "When Harry Met Sally" and "Fatal Attraction." Dating services, night courses, and self-help manuals used the figures to drum up business.

The trouble was, the figures were wrong. They were based on an outmoded premise—and on a questionable research methodology. Bennett and his colleagues reckoned that baby boom college-educated women faced a "marriage crunch," based on the assumption that women usually marry men an average of two or three years older than they are, who are more educated, and who have never been married before. The statistics showed that women born during the first half of the baby boom between 1945 and 1957 were going to find a shortage of men who were older, more educated, and who had never been married, in the less populated bracket of baby boys born during World War II. Women who waited to get their diplomas before they got married would find the pickings slim, the study predicted, because most of the eligible bachelors would have already been snapped up.

This dire prediction got enormous press, despite a contradictory study by Robert Schoen and John Baj at the University of Illinois in October of 1985 which concluded that the marriage squeeze in America was minimal.

In addition, Bennett, Bloom, and Craig based their findings on a sample from the 1982 Current Population Survey, an off-year in census data collection which included only 60,000 households. They then broke the sample down into even smaller subgroups.   The result was that they were making generalizations based on a very small, unrepresentative sample of women.

A U.S. Census Bureau demographer, Jeanne Moorman, challenged the Harvard-Yale findings. Using the official census figures and conventional standard-life tables, Moorman concluded that at 30, never-married college educated women had a 58 to 66 percent chance of marrying—three times the Harvard-Yale study's prediction.   At 35, the odds were 32 to 41 percent, seven times higher than the Harvard-Yale figure. And at 40, the chances were 17 to 23 percent, 23 times higher than Harvard-Yale figures.

Moorman also found that a 30-year-old single college educated woman was more likely to marry than a woman with only a high school education.

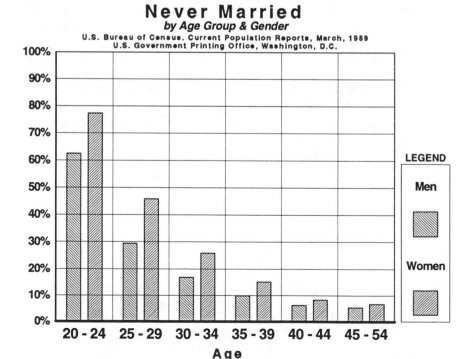

Never Married
by Age Group & Gender
U.S. Bureau of Census. Current Population Reports, March, 1989
U.S. Government Printing Office, Washington, D.C.

LEGEND

Men

Women

Age

Moorman pointed out that recent data showed that while the marriage rate has been declining in the general population, it has actually increased among women with four or more years of college education who marry between 25 and 45.

Statistics show that those who marry later have a lower probability of separation and divorce.   People who marry in their thirties, sixties, and seventies have a higher level of divorce than those who marry in their forties and fifties, according to Andrew Cherlin in his book, Marriage, Divorce, Remarriage.

The truth is that the proportion of unwed women is smaller than it has ever been.   Eight percent of women between 45 and 54 were single in 1950, but by 1985, it had dropped to only 5 percent. The median age of women living alone in 1986 was 66.

Almost every adult in the United States eventually marries. More than 90 percent of every generation on record has eventually married.   The generation born just after World War II has had the highest marriage rate ever—with 96.4 percent of the females and 94.1 percent of the males marrying.

Divorces per 100,000
by Age Group & Gender
U.S. Census Bureau, 1989, Statistical Abstracts of USA,
1991, 111th Edition, Washington, D.C.
4.708 million men & 6.678 million women

Some Overlooked Facts

Another misleading part about the Harvard-Yale study was that it left out divorced men. The truth is that the divorce rate in America is nearly 50 percent, and has been for almost two decades. Eighty percent of all divorced men remarry within three to five years of their divorce. Seventy-five percent of all divorced women also remarry. There are almost as many remarriages each year as there are first marriages. Forty-five percent of all marriages are remarriages. Step-families are fast becoming one of the most common forms of families in the United States. Only 27 percent of all families in California are intact nuclear families.

The Harvard-Yale study was also based on the premise that women want to marry up, and that they have to choose their mates from a pool of men who are two to three years older than they, and who make more money.

But the truth is that the average woman marries a man only 1.8 years older than she, according to the National Center for Health Statistics in 1987. What's more, one in five wives earns more than her husband.

As women become increasingly economically self-sufficient, they have a diminishing need to marry a good provider, and can choose a man for qualities that complement their own. Mother had to look for a man who could support her financially, and as her part of the bargain, she looked after his emotional needs. If today's woman can provide for herself, then she needs a man who meets her emotional needs as well as her mother met her father's needs.

The Option of Remaining Single

The increasing ability of women to be economically independent has made it more feasible for people to choose to remain single as a lifestyle. Changing social and cultural values have made it possible for singles to meet their sexual and social needs outside of marriage, and society has cooperated by offering housing, social activities, and a variety of material goods designed especially for singles, from cruise vacations to cans containing a single serving of soup.

During the 1970s, the number of men living alone rose by about 60 percent, while the number of women living alone increased about 40 percent. Single women have fewer drug and alcohol problems than single men. However, singles of both sexes report feeling lonely more often than married people do.

Some divorced women report that they feel happier single than they did when they were married, but that is not to say that they wouldn't be happier married to someone other than their previous spouse.

Holly, 32, was briefly married in her early twenties. Following her divorce she had a series of relationships with men who couldn't keep their jobs and relied on her for financial support. She said she was happier when she wasn't in a relationship, because she didn't like the caretaker role that she had found herself in during all of her relationships.   She liked the freedom and autonomy of the single life, and not having to report back to another person who she experienced as controlling.

Kay, 47, was married for 18 years and has been single for the past seven. She says that while she enjoys having a steady man in her life for companionship and for sex, she really prefers living alone.

"I like to be able to stay up late at night and read or watch television without worrying that I am disturbing someone else, and not having to worry about rushing home from work to see to it that someone else's dinner is cooked," she said. "I can tend to my own needs without having to worry about anyone else. I can buy a mauve sofa if I want to, or paint the bedroom fuchsia, and I don't have to be concerned with whether or not another person shares my tastes."

Kay also says that during the years she has been single, she has made some close male friends, with whom she has warm platonic relationships.

"There's one man I go to art galleries with, and another I horseback ride with," she said.   "When I was married, my ex-husband was jealous if I had relationships like that. I like to be able to see both men and women without having to worry about whether or not it upsets anyone else."

Finding a Man for the 90s

While the single lifestyle has become more satisfying, most women do not choose to avoid romantic relationships entirely. Women generally want mates. One reason why many women who delayed marriage to forge a career have problems finding an appropriate mate is not because there aren't any men out there, but because they were socialized to look for the same kind of man their mothers married. Early marriages or serious entanglements may have gone awry because both the man and the woman tried to imitate the traditional complementary relationship modeled by their parents and popular culture, which may be too rigid and inflexible for this transitional generation.   If, as Gloria Steinem has suggested, the modern woman herself became the kind of man her mother married, then she needs to be looking for a very different kind of mate. Many women are still searching in the 1990s for a 1950s kind of guy.

Marital Status of the Population

AGE	Number of Men (in thousands)				
	Single	Married	Widowed	Divorced	Total
18 - 19 Years Old	3,533	95	2	5	3,635
20 - 24 Years Old	6,915	1,912	6	105	8,939
25 - 29 Years Old	4,890	5,243	-	518	10,650
30 - 34 Years Old	2,789	7,157	23	842	10,811
35 - 39 Years Old	1,461	7,091	33	1,009	9,595
40 - 44 Years Old	673	6,432	38	943	8,086
45 - 54 Years Old	801	9,661	164	1,291	11,917
55 - 64 Years Old	563	8,385	328	812	10,088
65 - 74 Years Old	386	6,387	704	402	7,880
75 Years Old & over	184	2,915	982	118	4,199
Total for All Men	22,195	55,279	2,282	6,044	85,799

AGE	Number of Women (in thousands)				
	Single	Married	Widowed	Divorced	Total
18 - 19 Years Old	3,366	333	8	11	3,719
20 - 24 Years Old	5,838	3,231	11	256	9,336
25 - 29 Years Old	3,184	6,755	31	858	10,827
30 - 34 Years Old	1,854	7,868	67	1,161	10,950
35 - 39 Years Old	969	7,391	133	1,281	9,775
40 - 44 Years Old	530	6,311	250	1,327	8,418
45 - 54 Years Old	692	9,518	697	1,798	12,705
55 - 64 Years Old	492	7,716	2,035	1,067	11,311
65 - 74 Years Old	441	5,251	3,614	560	9,867
75 Years Old & over	410	1,819	4,646	203	7,077
Total for All Women	17,775	56,195	11,492	8,522	93,984

Marriages & Divorces from 1960 to 1987

Year	Marriages	Divorces	% of Divorces
1960	8.5	2.2	26%
1970	10.6	3.5	33%
1980	10.6	5.2	49%
1987	9.9	4.8	48%

Source: U.S. Bureau of Census, Statistical Abstracts of the US, 1991, 111th Edition, Washington, D.C. 1991

After graduation from high school, Marilyn enrolled in an all-women's Catholic college, and during her first semester, attended a football weekend at an all-men's college. At a party on Saturday night, a thin, blue-eyed senior approached the 18-year-old Marilyn and asked her to dance.

"I'm an M.D.A.," he told her. "That stands for Medical-Doctor-Almost."

Mike Sweeney was good-looking, charming, and had big plans. He courted Marilyn long-distance until he graduated, and then enrolled in a medical school near her college. They were married right after her graduation, and she moved into his dormitory room. When their first daughter was born, they turned a dresser drawer into a bassinet for her.

Marilyn had become Mrs. Mike Sweeney—the fulfillment of every girlish dream she ever had.

For the next few years, Marilyn cooked, cleaned, and held menial part-time jobs as a restaurant hostess or a nursery school aide to make ends meet and help Mike get through his internships and residency. With their four children, they moved to the west coast, where Mike started a practice. He worked long hours and was gone until late at night, but Marilyn didn't complain. This was the way she had expected life to be. Men were supposed to go out and work hard and earn money, and women were supposed to stay home and take care of the babies and the house. For years they had to scrimp and save, and then Mike became very successful.

Being Mrs. Mike Sweeney in a town where her husband was a prominent doctor was a very big deal for Marilyn. Like her mother before her, she devoted her spare time to volunteering. She was a member of a group called "Doctors' Wives" who raised money for the local hospital. All of their friends were doctors and their wives.

Then, when Mike turned 39, he bought himself a flashy red sports car and began an affair with his receptionist. Marilyn was frantic. She bought new clothes, got a new hair-do, went on a diet. She lit candles in the bedroom, served champagne, did everything she could think of to win him back.

She cried and accused him of cheating on her; he denied it. She flirted and was coquettish; he laughed at her.

She didn't tell any of her friends what was happening. After all, lots of men cheated on their wives, got it out of their systems, and came back home. That's what she thought Mike would do, and she was prepared to forgive and forget. But Mike left Marilyn, divorced her, and married the receptionist.

Marilyn's world fell apart. Her friends urged her to get on with her life, but as far as Marilyn was concerned, she didn't have one. Her whole identity was wrapped up in being Mrs. Someone Else. When that identity was taken from her, she wasn't anyone at all.

Other people saw her as a pretty blonde woman in her late thirties with a nice house, four nice kids, and a whole life ahead of her. She saw herself as an empty shell. Marilyn had married before she had an identity of her own and had never forged one outside of her marriage.

Traditionally, women have conceptualized themselves in terms of someone else. They are someone's daughter, someone's sister, someone's friend, someone's sweetheart, someone's wife, someone's mother. Even women who had jobs often identified themselves first in terms of their relationships and only as an afterthought in terms of their jobs.

"I'm Joe's wife, Stevie's mom. Oh, and I'm a graphic artist."

Pre-Identity Relationships

Women who marry early—in their teens or early twenties, before they have developed a career or formed their own identity—usually are involved in Phase I or pre-identity relationships. These relationships typically follow the familiar format of the marriages of their parents, the complementary style of the 1950s. In these relationships, there is likely to be a division of jobs or roles according to gender—the man's work is paramount and the wife is in charge of keeping the home fires burning. The husband has greater status and control, in essence enacting a one-up, one-down relationship.

Women who delay marriage into their thirties and forties, on the other hand, who have built a career and formulated a personal identity, and women who have been married once or twice before and who are looking for a new relationship later in life, are likely to find more satisfaction in a Phase II or post-identity relationship. These relationships are characterized by a symmetrical sharing of roles and power. They reflect more equality and more negotiation in resolution of differences.

Denise: From Blank Slate to Whole Chapter

Denise, now 47, met Douglas during their freshman year at college. He was tall and skinny, with shiny blue-black hair and an engaging smile. Denise thought he was one of the most intelligent men she had ever met, and she liked his sense of humor. But more than that, she was impressed by what he told her he planned to do with his life. He wanted to go to law school, and hoped someday to run for Congress. Marrying him meant moving a great distance from her family, because he intended to return to his home state to attend law school, but Denise felt that the life he was offering to share with her would be exciting. If she married Douglas, she'd be a lawyer's wife. They would live in San Francisco at first, and if he got elected to Congress, they'd live in Washington, D.C. To Denise, it seemed that her future would be financially secure and filled with exciting possibilities—different from what she viewed as her home-maker mother's more humdrum existence. By marrying Douglas, she hitched her wagon to his star.

Denise had grown up in a traditional 50s household. She was born during World War II, while her father was overseas. Her mother worked as a schoolteacher, but quit her job the very day her husband came home from the war. Henceforth, Denise's father brought home the bacon and her mother cooked it. When Denise came home from school, her mother was always there with milk and cookies.

Although Denise was as good a student as Douglas in college, she never gave any thought to applying to graduate school. Imme-diately after graduation, she followed Douglas to the city where he had been accepted to law school, and got a job. At the end of Douglas' first year in law school, right after final exams, they were quietly married by a justice of the peace.

Denise really liked her job, and she was good at it. She had always expected that she would quit as soon as Douglas established his practice and devote herself to raising children, as her mother had. But as she approached her late twenties, she had a hard time imagining staying home all day. When their first child was born, she adored the baby, but was bored at home with no adult com-pany.

Denise went back to school, got a graduate degree, and em-barked on a career while her children were still toddlers. As the years went by, she became more and more successful at her work. While Douglas took pride in her career, and enjoyed the fact that other people viewed Denise as an accomplished woman, he believed that his work came first.

"I don't mind if you work," he frequently told her, "but you can't let it interfere with my work." That meant that when one of the children was sick, Denise was the one to stay home, not Douglas. They both worked from 9 a.m. to 5 p.m., but when she finished work, Denise picked up the children at the day care center, hurried home, and got dinner on the table while Douglas read the mail, mixed a cocktail, and perused the newspaper. After dinner, he took a shower and settled down in front of the television set while she loaded the dishwasher, supervised the children's homework and baths, and got them tucked into bed. On Saturdays, Douglas frequently worked in his office, while Denise shopped for dinner parties to entertain his clients. She took vacation time from her job to go along with him on his business trips.

Denise and Douglas had a traditional, complementary marriage. As the years went by, there was also increasing tension and stress between them as they took increasingly polarized positions on every issue on which they differed. After 18 years of marriage, they were divorced. At 41, Denise found herself single again. The thought of dating again terrified her at first, but once she got into the swing of it, she found she really liked it.

"When I married Douglas, I was like a blank sheet of paper," she told a friend. "By choosing him, I also chose in what part of the country I would live, the socioeconomic bracket in which I would be, and so much else of who I would be. What he did with his life determined mine, to a huge extent. Since he was financially successful, I had an affluent lifestyle, traveled to foreign countries, and met interesting people. If he had been unsuccessful, my life would have been less fortunate. I was lucky in my choice of him—even though the marriage didn't last—because he provided me with the interesting lifestyle I had hoped that he would. I just as easily could have wound up marrying a man who had big dreams but didn't realize them. Marrying a man in his twenties is really like getting a pig in a poke."

Denise went on to outline how dating in her forties was different from what it was like when she was in her twenties.

"Now, I'm not a blank slate. I'm a whole chapter. I have a job, a career, an identity of my own. I already own a home, a car, and have children. I don't need to find a man to support me, or to give me children. I can take care of myself and of them, too, thank you very much. Now I can just look for a man who is a good companion, who I enjoy being with, and who adds something interesting and valuable to my life."

Denise pointed out that when she dated men in their forties, she knew more of what she was getting into than she had in her twenties. "When I married Doug, he had big plans, but I had no way of knowing whether or not he would realize them. I also had no way of telling whether or not he would be a good husband, and I certainly didn't know how good a father he would be. Nobody has any idea what it is like to be a parent until they have been one, so there isn't any way to tell if a man is going to be a good dad, no matter how well-intentioned he may seem.

"But when I go out with divorced men in their forties, I can see from what they say about their ex-wives and their marriages a lot about how they view marriage. The good ones have learned something from their mistakes too. I can see how interested they are in their children, and how much time they devote to them. And of course, by the time a man is in his forties, he has either proved that he is going to be a success in his career, or he hasn't been. Not only am I a fully developed human being now, but the men I go out with are, too."

Life Stages

Just as children are thought to go through "stages"—such as the "terrible twos" and the "noisy nines"—the prevailing wisdom has been that adulthood is a series of predictable stages. In the "All the world's a stage" speech from *As You Like It*, Shakespeare describes seven stages of a man's life: beginning with a "mewing infant," moving on to the "whining schoolboy"... to "the lover sighing like a furnace," "a soldier full of strange oaths," "and then the justice...full of wise saws." In the sixth stage of life, old age, Shakespeare says a man "shifts into the lean and slippered pantaloon with spectacles on nose and pouch on side." "In the last scene of all," he says, "that ends this strange and eventful history is second childishness and mere oblivion, sans teeth, sans eyes, sans taste, sans everything."

A couple of hundred years later, a Viennese psychologist, Else Frenkel-Brunswik, picked up Shakespeare's cue in looking at adulthood as a series of predictable changes. She culled the biographies of 400 historical figures, including Queen Victoria, Leo Tolstoy, and John D. Rockefeller, and in 1936 published a study narrowing down the stages of human life to five.

Most recent theories about the stages of adult life are based on the work of psychologist Erik H. Erikson, who published his first book, *Childhood and Society*, in 1950. Erikson believed that life is lived in stages, and that each stage presents a predictable crisis characteristic of the issues of that particular stage of life. Erikson described each primary crisis that occurs during each of the important stages of life. He defined a crisis not as a catastrophe, but as a turning point, or a fork in the road.

According to Erikson, the primary task during the first of three stages of adult life is to achieve intimacy. During the next stage, the primary task is generativity, including both the rearing of one's own children and the passing on of wisdom to the next generation. In the final stage of maturity, the task is integrity.

Erikson wrote that while young men achieve an identity before they form an intimate attachment, women hold back forming an identity.

"The stage of life crucial for the emergence of an integrated female identity is the step from youth to maturity, the state when the young woman, whatever her work career, relinquishes the care received from her parental family in order to commit herself to the love of a stranger and to the care to be given to his and her offspring," Erikson wrote in *Women and Inner Space*.

Erikson goes on to say, "Young women often ask whether they can 'have an identity' before they know whom they will marry and for whom they will make a home. Granted that something in the young woman's identity must keep itself open for the peculiari-

Erikson's Eight Stages of Life		
Lifestage	**Value**	**Conflict**
Infancy	Hope	Basic trust vs. mistrust
Early childhood	Will	Autonomy vs. shame & doubt
Play age	Purpose	Initiative vs. guilt
School age	Competence	Industry vs. inferiority
Adolescence	Fidelity	Identity vs. role confusion
Young Adulthood	Love	Intimacy vs. isolation
Maturity	Care	Generativity vs. stagnation
Old Age	Wisdom	Integrity vs. despair

ties of the man to be joined and of the children to be brought up, I think that much of a young woman's identity is already defined in her kind of attractiveness and in the selective nature of her search for the man (or men) by whom she wishes to be sought. This, of course, is only the psychosexual aspect of her identity, and she may go far in postponing its closure while training herself as a worker and a citizen and while developing as a person within the role possibilities of her time."

What Erikson meant was that women need to put part of their identity on hold until they decide whom to marry and then they adopt part of his identity as their own. He also quite specifically said that when women prepare for careers, they delay the psychosexual part of their identities. Rather than formulating an identity around their work itself, they remain partially formed people. It seems as though Erikson didn't anticipate the lifestyles of women in the 1990s. His concept of female identity still hinged on the completion myth that "without a man, a woman is nothing."

During the 1960s and 1970s, a Yale psychologist, Daniel Levinson, studied adult men and concluded that adults mature through various stages, each with its own specific tasks and goals. Levinson concluded that a man needs to complete the jobs in each stage before he is ready to move on to the next. Most men, he found, work through each stage in a maximum of seven or eight years.

At about the same time that Levinson was conducting his studies, Roger Gould, a psychiatrist at the University of California, Los Angeles, was interviewing white, middle-class men and women about the predictable stages in their lives. Author Gail Sheehy described these stages in her 1976 best-selling popular-psychology book, *Passages*, which brought life development theories to the attention of the general public.

Sheehy explained that the task of young adults in their twenties is to prepare for their life's work, to find a mentor if possible, and to establish an intimate bond with a member of the opposite sex. Men are expected to finish their educations, begin a career, and find a wife.   In their thirties, men are supposed to be consumed with their careers, climbing the corporate ladder, or establishing themselves in their profession.   Woman's work during their twenties and thirties, according to this model, is to bear children.

During the mid-thirties to mid-forties, according to Sheehy, most adults reassess their progress and accomplishments, causing some men to go through "mid-life crises" and precipitating divorces among couples who felt the choices they made in their twenties wouldn't hold up for the long haul.

By their mid-forties, Sheehy found, most men had come to terms with themselves, resigning themselves to whatever degree of success they had already achieved.   Men who asked, "Is that all there is?" began to accept the fact that it probably was.   For most women, the mid-forties was a time when children were leaving the nest.   Many of them went back to work or established new careers outside of the home.

One of the things that Sheehy pointed out was that "It was glaringly obvious that the tempo of development is not synchronized in the sexes.   The fundamental steps of expansion that will open a person, over time, to the full flowering of his or her individuality are the same for both genders.   But men and women are rarely in the same place struggling with the same questions at the same age."

Sheehy continued, "During the twenties, when a man gains confidence by leaps and bounds, a married woman is usually losing the superior assurance she once had as an adolescent.   When a man passes 30 and wants to settle down, a woman is often becoming restless.   And just at the point around 40, when a man feels himself to be standing on a precipice, his strength, power, dreams, and illusions slipping away beneath him, his wife is likely to be brimming with ambition to climb her own mountains."

But as Laurie Levin and Laura Golden Belotti point out in their 1992 book, *You Can't Hurry Love*, "A lot has changed since 1976, when Sheehy's book was first published.   Her 'stages' apply almost exclusively to the parents of baby boomers, those who preceded the advent of feminism, counterculture, and the economic squeeze of the 1970s." Life-stage theorist Roger Gould told Levin and Belotti he has rethought these issues and now considers the stages of life as more of a continuum.

"Rather than seeing adult development as a straight line, many sociologists now propose that adults reach maturity via a number of alternative routes.   They argue that life is much more haphazard, that developmental 'tasks' don't happen to everyone on cue," Belotti and Levin wrote.

Most of the collective wisdom about how human beings form their identities, and about how normal human beings progress though adulthood, is based on studies of men, and on the premise that what is normal for men is normal for everyone. If women aren't like men, then they are considered to be deviating from the norm. In an era when most women work outside the home and most households have two breadwinners, theories about identity and self-worth will change inevitably, also.

Anchoring Relationships

"Vive la difference," is what the French say, acknowledging the differences between men and women. And there are fundamental differences.

Whether it is because of conditioning, modeling, or biological imperative, women do more nurturing in our society. They tend to spend more of their lifetimes addressing issues of relationships and tending to the needs of others.

As a result, their concept of themselves is more other-directed than men's. Rather than seeing themselves as a solo act, women tend to see themselves within a web of connections. They view their relationships as anchor points in their concept of who they are: a woman is someone's daughter, someone's sister, someone's sweetheart, someone's wife, someone's mother. It has only been relatively recently that women have thought of themselves in connection with a further identity—that of a lawyer, a doctor, an accountant, or a real estate broker.

Our culture defines maturity as the ability to move away from home, to separate from parents, and to be self-sufficient. The ultimate accomplishment for a man in growing up is to cut the apron strings; to be separate. Freud even defined the ego as "something autonomous and unitary, marked off distinctively from everything else."

Yet, autonomy is not a universal value for women. The value for women is to be good caretakers and to be responsible for others. While a good man is autonomous, a good woman takes good care of others.

Women today find themselves in a double bind, because many of the traits considered desirable in a mature man, such as competitiveness and aggression, are considered inappropriate in a woman. While aggression is sanctioned in men, women are criticized for being too pushy. Yet if she is passive, she is considered masochistic and a victim.

Psychologists say that by the time little girls become women, they have developed significant feelings of inferiority because feminine traits of nurturing and receptivity are not valued by the culture. Autonomy is valued but interrelatedness is not.

Psychologist Ruthellen Josselson concluded that identity for women is more complicated than it is for men, because women need to try to balance their aspirations with their relationships to other people, and their personal relationships usually come first. Because women see themselves within a web of connectedness to others, maintaining those connections is valuable to women. The ability to function as a networker is a factor in a woman's identity in a way that it is not in a man's.

Because a woman's sense of who she is tends to be embedded in relationships, it is not until she is in her mid-thirties that she develops a primary identity, a consistent and stable notion of who she is. Identity encompasses who one is and who one is not, and includes one's values, status, biological characteristics, and social roles.

Erikson saw identity as an "amalgam" of certain givens—such as gender, temperament, physical attributes, limitations stemming from psychosexual development, gender ideation, and social roles. In other words, a woman may think of herself as a pretty, blue-eyed blonde too short to be a model—and that is part of who she is. Part of her self-concept also encompasses her notion of what a woman is in society—a wife, a mother, a caretaker. Only recently has her career role become another identity attribute.

As recently as the mid 1980s, Josselson reported that interviews she conducted with women when they were 22 years old, and then again when they were in their early thirties, indicated that women really hadn't changed much since the 1950s. In her 1987 book, *Finding Herself*, Josselson concluded that most women still anchored their identities in their husbands, their families, and their children. Even working women did not identify themselves primarily by their career. But most of the women Josselson interviewed had not had working mothers as models to emulate. Women who had a female mentor tended to identify themselves more in terms of their careers. As more young women are reared by working mothers as role models, more women will tend to identify with their careers.

A study commissioned by *Cosmopolitan* Magazine in 1980, published in 1986, predicted that women in the future would spend a larger percentage of their lives being single than any generation that preceded them. Because of the later age at which most women marry, the high divorce rate, and women's newly found ability to be economically self-sufficient, the Batelle Group, which conducted the study, concluded that women will emerge with a primary identity separate from their traditional roles as wives and mothers. At best, women are in a transitional phase, and most career-minded women still want a relationship, but not to take on a man's identity. They have their own. Rather, they wish to be in a relationship in which they are valued and loved. Many also want to marry because they want to be mothers. Stage theorists such as Erikson, and others who have popularized their ideas such as Gail Sheehy and

Daniel Levinson, wrote about life transitions before seeing the effects of the Women's Movement of the 1960s and 1970s filter down on a collective level.

Mythologist Joseph Campbell suggested that men and women spend the first half of their lives dealing with identity and sexuality issues. It may well be that during the first 35 years of life, while men are finding an identity, women have been too busy having babies and taking care of other people to find out who they are or are capable of being outside of these roles. For women who marry young and have children in their twenties, it is not until they are past their child-bearing years that they have a chance to develop primary identities of their own. Women who delay marriage in favor of careers build their identities before they formulate intimate relationships, much in the same way men do.

The problem is to what extent women honor their relationships above themselves, and hence fuse their personal needs into the relationship? Do they squelch their own voices and keep their opinions to themselves in order to maintain relationships? Or worse, do they deny themselves any opinion as a way of handling their conflict between autonomy and relationships? Or do they work out a way of honoring those competing loyalties to themselves and others? All these questions remain open.

Factors or Attributes in Identity
Consistent notion of self
Ego differentiation/who one is not
Values
Peer relationship or status
Social role
Sexual identity
Psychosexual aspects of development influenced by early traumatic events
Gender identity
Interests
Significant identification with others
Natural talents
Physical attributes
Genetic aspects of temperament

The Masculine and Feminine Sides

The ability to penetrate, separate, take charge, initiate, create, stand firmly and to articulate are considered masculine characteristics. Feminine characteristics are to be caring, to be nurturing, to be concerned about feelings.   Both men and women have masculine and feminine sides to their personalities.   To the extent that a woman is competent and has authority, she is drawing on her masculine side.

Psychologist Carl G. Jung called the feminine side the anima and the masculine side the animus.   A woman's animus is described as the unconscious masculine side of her personality. Most women initially identify consciously with the feminine side, and unconsciously exclude their masculine.   (Men do the reverse.) Part of a woman's identity is consciously claimed and part is unconscious.

In the 1950s model of relationships, women acted out the unconscious masculine side of their personalities through the men in their lives.   Instead of being assertive themselves, they found men to be aggressive for them.   Instead of slaying dragons themselves, they found men to do it for them.   The same principle operated for men. They found women to enact their feminine side; to be in charge of their relationships and to do the nurturing in their lives.

Marty & Ingrid:
Playing the Mother & Father Role to Each Other

Marty was an engineer.   He was very orderly, very logical, a good provider.   Ingrid, a nursery school teacher, married him because he seemed like someone who could take good care of her. Unconsciously, he was a father figure to her, a good daddy who would love her no matter what and be there when she needed him.

What Marty liked about Ingrid was that she seemed to understand him.   He felt that they were connected in a non-verbal way, that she knew instinctively what he was feeling.   She was nurturing and reminded him subliminally of his mother.

After two years of marriage, Marty was disgusted with Ingrid. He was tired of having to take care of her all the time.   Why couldn't she figure things out for herself? If she was smart enough to teach school, why did she have to ask him everything? Why did she have to act so dumb? He no longer felt that she understood what he needed.   He resented the fact that if he wanted something, he had to tell her.

Marty was projecting onto Ingrid his own unconscious feminine side, and she was projecting onto him her own unconscious masculine side.   Both of them were expecting the other to complete them. Ingrid wanted him to be her father.   He wanted her to be his perfect woman, a combination of his mother and a sexual fantasy figure, like a Playboy bunny. She expected him to handle her cognitive functions, to do her thinking for her, and he expected her to take the nurturing roles for both of them.

After counseling, Ingrid learned to make some decisions on her own, and Marty started asking her for what he wanted.

Exercise:

Take a sheet of paper and make a list of qualities you would expect to find in the ideal mate. Is this man passive or aggressive? Is he powerful? Is he nurturing? What position does he occupy in the world? How does he carry himself? What is important to him?

What most women find is that they have described their own unconscious masculine qualities. Women frequently look for men who look like their underdeveloped side, but projecting these qualities onto a man has some specific pitfalls.

Second-Half-of-Life Issues

Before the age of 35, people deal with issues about who they are and their own sexuality. During the second half of life, we are concerned with sorting out issues about our selves and our relationship to the whole. Carl G. Jung thought that the task of the second half of life was to integrate the unconscious parts of our personality. For a man, the unconscious side is his feminine side—his emotionality. For a woman, the unconscious side is her masculine side, the part that is competent and deals with the outer world.

Particularly during the first half of life, many women deal with their masculine side by choosing to relate to men who enact their masculine side for them. Other women live out their masculine sides themselves, and repress their feminine side. It seems to be difficult for women to balance the two sides during the first half of life. Either their career works, or their marriage works. Few manage to strike a good balance and have both work at the same time.

However, in their thirties and forties, women begin to identify their own positions and values independent of the men in their lives. Instead of seeing authority as a projected quality which men possess, it begins to be related to their concept of self.

Much of what we consider to be traditional female development is what Jane Loevinger referred to in her book, *Ego Development*, as the conformist stage, in which one is striving for approval and acceptance. When one feels accepted, one experiences high self-esteem. The problem with deriving a sense of self-esteem from a sense of being accepted is that a woman feels a loss of identity when a relationship ends. Within the relationship she is unable to successfully argue or negotiate fair compromises because she fears they threaten the security of the relationship—and part of her identity.

During the second half of life, women often turn from dealing with more feminine issues—such as mothering—to developing the more masculine sides of their personalities. One challenge at this stage of life is to achieve a balance between their femininity and masculinity.

Mary Jean got married when she was 22. She was content to bask in her husband's aura. She let him make most of the decisions, and essentially molded her life around him. After three children and seven years of marriage, she felt dissatisfied with her life and talked her husband into going into counseling with her.

Her therapist helped her see how she was giving herself away. He encouraged her to get a job and a focus for herself. In the process, she ran into conflict with her husband, whose idea of a couple was for the woman to defer to the decisions of the man. Needless to say, Mary Jean needed to have enough strength to carry through with her convictions and to see if her husband adapted to the changes. If he didn't, their relationship would be headed for divorce court.

The last thirty years have witnessed a collective shift in how women see themselves. Many women now struggle to know themselves and their own opinions as well as the opinion of the men in their lives. Competence is more integrated for women who have succeeded in their careers. A group of career women interviewed in 1987, all professors, psychologists, or teachers, did not view themselves as part of the prevailing power structure, but all of them said that their sense of their own competence and authority had increased since their adolescent years.

As a result of feminism, more women collectively identify with their competence. Although there are still women who imbue men with authority, and there are those who spend most of their lives attempting to be the ideal male fantasy, clearly there are many others who have managed to integrate competence, authority, *and* femininity into their sense of self. Having an internal locus of control is related to better personal development, higher self-esteem, and a greater sense of self-determination. In the 1990s an increasing number of women have shifted their locus of control from an external to an internal reference point. It may still be that in the first half of life, women still rely on others for their sense of self-esteem, guidance, sense of competence, and strength, but it appears that there is a shift in the second half of life to a more internal center of power.

The Role of Biology and Hormones

There are many theories explaining sexual roles. Some theorists suggest that roles are related to biological traits. Others define roles as primarily economically driven. Still others see roles as the product of social interactions. In most societies, the division of labor is gender-related.

Stereotypes about gender have maximized the differences between the sexes. Men are seen as competent and women are seen as fearing competence. The 1990s is a time of fluctuating roles, a time of stretching the bonds that tie role to gender. The men and women interviewed for this book seemed to be more aware of both the masculine and feminine sides of themselves, which may mean conceptions of masculine and feminine are changing.

We appear at the end of the twentieth century to be in a period of transition about values. The roles in which men and women find themselves differ enormously from the notions of women who were raised in the 1950s and 1960s. Because of this, what people need in a mate has also changed.

Do You Want A Man Like Dear Old Dad?

In the past, when women married right out of high school, or without ever having lived apart from their childhood home, they were unlikely to have formed an identity of their own. Whether they were holding identities in abeyance, as the theorists who based their notions on Erikson suggested, or whether they were projecting their unconscious masculine sides onto men, most wives entered into complementary relationships based on the need for completion.

The 1950s pattern of relationships mostly hinge on this notion of completion; neither party is whole without the other. Together they form a conglomerate identity. The traits and roles played out within these relationships are complementary; one person is dominant and the other recessive. One person thinks and the other one feels. Complementary relationships exaggerate the differences between two people. Many marriages today are still based on this model, which does still work for many people who have traditional values and roles.

In a 1950s style marriage, both partners adhere to a structured and clearly defined set of role expectations and subsequent division of labor. The woman, even if she also works outside the home, still sees the household and the children as her primary responsibilities. The power relationship is unequally balanced and favors the one who brings in the larger income, which in 80 percent of all families is still the man.

Unfortunately, this complementary style tends to become rigid. Many women and men in complementary relationships end up feeling disillusioned and unfulfilled.

As exemplified by Beth, the plastic surgeon who chose a man in a very different field for her second husband, relationships formed after the woman has developed an identity for herself, through her career or other life experiences, tend to be very different from pre-identity relationships. These post-identity relationships—delayed or second marriages—hinge around a whole set of different assumptions based on egalitarian values and more flexibility in roles. The task for these couples is to negotiate and renegotiate what the relationship is going to look like. A principle in these relationships is a more equal distribution of power and control. Flexibility and adaptability are the characteristics that mark successful symmetrical relationships.

Despite the radical changes many career women have experienced, many continue to select men like their fathers. If they look for a man like their father, they are going to wind up with a marriage like their mother's—the 1950s style complementary marriage in which the man is king.

Many women have not found the right man because they are still looking with the wrong formula in mind. Older, taller, richer, smarter works if you want to be traditional, but for women who want to marry laterally, a new set of criteria needs to be part of their shopping list. Women who have found an identity for themselves are ready to look for a man who is an equal, not just to be taken care of, but to be valued and loved.

CHAPTER THREE

Romance & Chemistry

Love demands the impossible, the absolute,
the sky on fire, the inexhaustible springtime,
life after death, and death itself transfigured
into eternal life.

—**Albert Camus**

$\mathcal{I}$n the Rodgers and Hammerstein musical, "South Pacific," the hero sings, "Some enchanted evening, you will meet a stranger...across a crowded room...and somehow you'll know, you'll know even then, that somewhere you'll see her again and again." The song goes on..."Who can explain it? Who can tell you why? Fools give you reasons; wise men never try."

Those romantic lyrics sum up what many people feel about falling in love. They believe that somewhere on earth there exists the perfect mate, and when they find that special someone, they will magically recognize him, and that the attraction will be mystical and inexplicable. They will live happily ever after, because true love conquers all.

That is the collective mythology on romantic love. The truth is that couples get along well together and stay together because of a variety of ingredients in their relationship—a mix of psychological development, similar or complementary life scripts and ideas about roles, and compatible traits, enhanced by good verbal and non-verbal communication, sexual compatibility, and good problem solving abilities. When all of these factors come together, the happy result is called intimacy—when everything feels harmonious and right between two people.

These things don't just happen automatically, and the way people meet is not just by chance, either. People pick each other out for specific reasons, some wise, some foolish, some conscious, and some unconscious. What are the best ways to choose a mate? Can you rely on chemistry? If not, how else can you choose a potential mate? Selecting is an individual process. No two people are identical in what they want.   But many women, when asked what they are looking for, say, "I'm looking for someone with whom the chemistry is right." Unfortunately, this is one of the worst criteria people use to choose a mate. The main ingredients of this magical formula tend to be physical appearance and the physiological reaction it elicits within them. Do your hormones go raging when you look at him? Does your heart palpitate and do your palms sweat just anticipating his arrival? It's a feeling most people have experienced, and it can be intoxicating.

The problem with choosing people this way is that your associations and your projections about the person may have nothing to do with who the person really is, much less whether you are compatible with him.   Both chemistry and its cousin, romantic love, are based largely upon projection.

When you are physically attracted to someone, your body chemistry changes.   You have the same aroused response as when you are frightened or need to protect yourself.   Adrenaline surges through your bloodstream, your heart rate increases, saturating your muscles with oxygen-rich blood; your palms may sweat, your face may flush, and you feel excited.   This is the physical reaction many people equate with falling in love.

It is the opposite reaction from the relaxation response when you feel safe and secure.   When you are calm, your body releases norepinephrine, slowing the heart rate, directing the blood to the organs and the extremities, and giving you an overall sense of well-being.   This is a much more boring state, not nearly as exciting as the being-in-love feeling.

Romantic Love

In our culture, romantic love is portrayed as a near-religious experience.   You are supposed to experience merger, have an automatic best friend, be supplied with spontaneous erotic sexual expression, intellectual stimulation, and a steady date for New Year's Eve, all rolled up into one person.

This concept of romantic love comes straight out of European literature, from lyric poems about knights in shining armor during the Middle Ages. The 12th Century troubadours described chivalric love, with its erotic aspects spiritualized, as a noble, almost holy passion.

During the Middle Ages, marriage was usually a business arrangement, and partners did not choose their spouses.   So the courtly lover was usually a bachelor knight pining for another man's wife, like the doomed Tristan and Isolde, and Sir Lancelot and Lady Guinevere.   The lover swore allegiance to his lady love, and demonstrated his dedication to her by his nobility on the crusades and in knightly battles.   But the courtly lover never actually got the girl, certainly never married her, and they never had to squabble over a joint checking account or who was going to carry out the garbage.   And they never had sex.

The concept of courtly love was intertwined with feudalism, with the lover playing the role of servant to the lady of the manor. Metaphorically, the knight also served the God of Love. Other writers linked romantic love to Christian ethics, with the lady worshipped from afar by a lover who repents his sins. By pledging fidelity to the lady, he earned his right to be admitted to heaven through her grace.

Historians aren't certain whether medieval courtly love was a fiction, or whether it really reflected the way things were among the aristocracy in medieval times. However, no matter whether it was truth or fiction, the concept of the ennobling power of love as the ultimate experience in life has affected how people have viewed love ever since.

The difference between us and the poets of the 12th Century is that we fully expect to find romantic love and have it transform ourselves and our lover.   We wait patiently for the knight in shining armor, who will surely make the house payments on time and won't ever lose his hair or begin to snore.

In the 12th century, no one expected to marry the romantic lover or have great sex with him for the next 40 or 50 years. Now we have turned a literary and mythical ideal into hopes for reality, and think we can have it all, all rolled up in one person.

In his book *We*, Robert Johnson wrote, "Romantic love is not love but a complex of attitudes about love's involuntary feelings, ideals, and reactions....   There is a notion that we are incomplete somehow and if we fall in love with this person and can own this person and have this person we are somehow greater than who we are as just a person."

Romantic love is more realistically viewed as one stage of a relationship.   Being able to fantasize about someone works best when you don't really know that person. Once you do, you have to choose between the real man and the fantasy.   In healthy relationships, when the initial projection begins to fade and the real person comes into focus, you find that person is someone you still love. If the real person is too different from your projections, the relationship usually ends.

Type = Chemistry + Romantic Love Projected

Chemistry for a certain "type" is not lust alone. That hunk over there may have a great build, but chances are the reason that you feel an attraction to him is because he reminds you of someone in your past with whom you had a connection. People frequently believe that this feeling comes out of nowhere, but generally you are attracted to a stranger because he or she reminds you of other positive or even negative associations in your past. Maybe it was sexual, or maybe it was emotional, but you recall some kind of bond. Maybe the man's smile reminds you of an old boyfriend, or he has a mustache like a favorite teacher in high school, or he has a volatile personality which reminds you of a negative but passionate love affair. The association of something familiar is very enticing. That is why people believe that there is a certain "type" they like. A man will say that he is attracted to petite blondes, or a woman will say that she likes surfer types and that a bald man with a paunch just isn't her type. Although Jeffrey Ullman, the founder of Great Expectations Dating Service, found that men relied on chemistry for their mate selection more than women, many women also reject men on the grounds that he "isn't my type."

"He's Not My Type"

Cindy, a court reporter, had above-average looks when she was in her twenties and early thirties. She always had plenty of boyfriends and it seemed that she could get any man she wanted. She was attracted to blue-eyed men who were well-muscled and had what she called "a twinkle in their eye." She liked athletic, outdoorsy men, and particularly skiers. She had a series of initially thrilling but ultimately unfulfilling liaisons with handsome ski bums who pursued her in the beginning, and then treated her badly. None of the men ever wanted a commitment, and eventually the relationships ended.

At 40, Cindy is still single, and she is anxious. Her friends have married and have had children, and she feels that life has passed her by. She likes her work, but not enough to build her life around it. She enjoys making pottery, but not enough to make it her mission. She's still attractive, but she no longer stops traffic. She can't figure out why the guys who are her type don't stick around and why she can't find a man to marry her. Her sister told her, "You need to start choosing a man on the basis of how he treats you instead of what he looks like." Her answer was that nice guys didn't turn her on. "They just aren't my type," Cindy insisted.

What do people mean when they say he or she is not their type? One of the strongest components of "type" is related to unfinished psychological business. A woman who has never felt that she was very pretty may try to date only extremely good-looking men, an unsuccessful or shy woman may only pick gregarious, aggressive men, and a woman with low self-esteem may pick a very critical man.   The daughters of alcoholics frequently select men who are substance abusers.

Fulfilling Your Script

Even more enticing than finding someone who reminds you physically or in other ways of someone you knew in the past is the sense that you have found someone who has a complementary set of expectations about what love feels like.

Another way of looking at matching types uses the concept of a script.   Sigmund Freud spoke of the need to repeat past scenarios. He called it "repetition compulsion."   In the 1970s, Eric Berne and Claude Steiner repackaged the idea in Transactional Analysis, explaining that people live their lives following scripts based on fundamental messages they learned about themselves as children. Falling in love, according to this theory, is what happens when two people realize that they have found someone with whom they can play out their life script.

Some psychologists say that most people can scan a crowded room and hone in within a matter of minutes on the one person there who can fulfill their script.   The initial recognition frequently feels magical, but what occurs after the magic wears off can be entangling and oppressive.   For a period of time, there is a heady, exciting feeling of falling in love.   After a time, however, reality sets in.   Often you find yourself feeling the way you felt in the past, enmeshed again in a relationship where you don't get what you need or you don't feel good about yourself.

Projection

You probably have had the experience of meeting a man and becoming overwhelmingly infatuated with him.   You thought about him constantly, lay awake at night thinking about him, wrote him letters or poems, and found ways to watch him from afar.   If you actually met him, or dated him, or even slept with him, at some point the bubble burst.   He wasn't what you expected.   In fact, he really wasn't very wonderful at all.   He was disappointing, maybe even annoying.

Jung explained the theory of projection by saying that couples fall in love when a woman finds a man who represents her unconscious masculine side, while simultaneously the man recognizes his unconscious feminine side in her.   This is a dual projective process. You project the familiar yet unconscious or unworked out part of you onto the face and the body of the other person, noticing all of their traits that go along with the projection, while ignoring the ones that don't.   He becomes brighter, richer, smarter than he is.

But something happens, and he fails to be your fantasy, and the real person appears. The real person, in fact, can be a distraction from your fantasy of who you want the person to be.

What made the fantasy so powerful was that it was a figment of your imagination. You used the man's body as a screen on which you projected your vision of the ideal lover. He was perfect, but he wasn't real.

In the Woody Allen movie, "The Purple Rose of Cairo," the heroine, played by Mia Farrow, fantasizes about a movie star who comes to life and steps off the screen and into her life. He is everything she ever dreamed of, but celluloid.

"But I don't exist," he eventually tells her, and she replies, "Well, nobody's perfect."

How To Tell If You Are Projecting

When a man projects his unconscious feminine side—or any of his other fantasies—onto you, it feels great initially. He thinks that you are the most beautiful woman he has ever met, the essence of femininity, and he adores you. You're on top of the world. But after awhile, it feels suffocating. You notice that he attributes some characteristics to you that you don't think you have and criticizes you when you differ from his image. He admires your patience, when actually you are rather short-tempered. He raves about your spaghetti sauce, when you just dumped it out of a jar. You get the sense that he doesn't really know you, and it's true. He doesn't. The sense of incongruity is the sign that a projection is coming your way.

On the other hand, you're projecting when you imagine that a man you've just met is absolutely perfect, a hero, your spiritual guide, and your ideal lover. You feel that he knows what it feels like to be you. You're totally in sync. Because he has a nice smile and listens attentively, you extrapolate that he is warm, tender and affectionate. Because he opened your car door, you assume that he is very courteous and caring. In fact, you interpret all data about him in the most positive way, and you ignore all the negative data.

If you are projecting, you have an unworldly fascination with the man, and can't stop thinking about him. There is a quality of compulsiveness about your feelings.

Love Junkies

For some people the intoxicating feeling of falling in love is more than a stage. It becomes the major theme of the relationship, and they remain caught up in the myth that they can find a perfect other half to make them whole. Traditional sex roles have reinforced this fantasy, for it is the codependent state that is cherished and celebrated in popular love mythologies.

Love junkies sometimes believe that they aren't in love if they aren't constantly in a state of excitement over the loved one. They cannot adjust to the relaxed, comfortable state of knowing someone well and feeling safe with them. They cannot stand to let the projective experience fade from a relationship.

Most relationships which start off with a feeling of falling in love involve some of the projective experience. It is the recognition that the two of you are similar in some ways that leads to the state of euphoria. Sometimes we manage to project our fantasies onto a worthwhile human being, and when the projection begins to fade, we still like the real person underneath. In a healthy relationship, the couple is able to make the transition into loving the real people, not just the fantasy.

The Fusion Fantasy:
"If He Really Loved Me, He'd ..."

An element of romantic mythology is the notion that when two people fall in love, they merge and become one with the other person. Each lover is expected to know what the other needs, and to be responsive to those needs, without being asked. If a man can't read his lover's mind, he has failed her.

The sense that two people in love are supposedly able to know instinctively what the other wants and to understand what would be pleasurable without being told is a fantasy. Sex is a common area for this mind-reading game, made more complicated by a social taboo against talking about sex. For those who expect their lovers to intuit what they want, the partner is in a perilous situation. He's supposed to be a mind-reader, and if he isn't, that means that the two of you aren't in sync. In reality, having to talk to your partner and tell him what you enjoy does not mean that something is missing in your relationship.

Everyone comes into a relationship with certain desires or needs; the degree of compulsiveness of these issues distinguishes between healthy and unhealthy relationships. Although everyone has some needs for bonding and being understood, for some people the neediness controls the relationship. When two relatively emotionally healthy people form a relationship, they should be capable of creating an interdependency, which in a strong relationship will nurture both of them. But where the relationship is formed around a need for fusion (driven by the need to make one or both parties whole) there is too much need and emotionality. Consequently, the relationship is prone to power struggles which are only partly resolved by one party losing his or her sense of self.

The problem with needing someone to this extent—for an entire identity—is that the couple cannot distinguish differences between themselves. Because they are driven to complete themselves through one another, they have little ability to tolerate differences. Invariably, in such tightly knit and dependent relationships, one person tries to control the other.

A healthy relationship is a source of sharing and respect for differences. A relationship based on fusion is seen by the participants as giving one or the other of them a source of self. Without the partner, the dependent one feels empty or without any purpose.

Some love songs romanticize the notion of fusion with lyrics that say essentially, "Without you, I'm nothing." For some this is a metaphor for how much they care about their partner; for others it is a literal expression of their neediness.

Fused relationships are problematic because the emotional need is so great that the failures of one person to provide what the other needs (in terms of mirroring, empathy, or the need to be in control) distress the individual so much that they may threaten the relationship. Hence, when one party disappoints the other, the conflict which results is intense and volatile.

Loretta, 32, was divorced, with a child she had abandoned to the care of her parents. She had been molested repeatedly by her stepfather during her adolescence so she was very distrustful of men. She met Paul, 39, who had also been abandoned as a child when his natural mother gave him to an orphanage.

On some very basic and primitive level, Paul thought of himself as unlovable and he never trusted love to last; he kept thinking he'd be abandoned again. Loretta, on the other hand, experienced men as lustful and out of control. Ambivalent about her sexuality, Loretta would be seductive only until Paul was aroused. When she had gotten the attention she wanted, she would turn him away, triggering his fear of abandonment.

Their conflicts escalated quickly, usually following her rejecting his sexual advances. Within minutes they would be in a heated fight that would often end in physical violence. Loretta would threaten to leave as the fight escalated; Paul would attempt to block her exit and she would fight back harder. Between these volatile quarrels, she would come on to him again, he would break his resolve not to see her; and they were back to square one. However, as is characteristic of this type of couples, the ante kept going up. Every time they went through this circular conflict, the intensity increased. It was their mutual dependency, not love, which kept them together. Even if such behavior is destructive, it feels so familiar that it is hard to leave.

Murray Bowen, a psychiatrist, suggested that couples who are fused like this work out their conflict in one of three ways. Loretta and Paul are examples of the first way—violent quarrels followed by periods of calm. This is typical with alcoholic couples and other couples who experience extreme dependency.

A second way in which such couples work out their conflict is through one of them becoming sick; the sick person controls the relationship with his illness. A third way is through unconsciously encouraging children to take sides with one parent. A parent shifts the fusion from between the couple to between the parent and the child, leaving the other parent as the outsider. The child is always the loser in this pattern, and frequently grows up wary of too much closeness, which he perceives as too engulfing.

Finding an Echo

One of our strongest needs in a relationship is the need to find an echo. The mythological god Narcissus only knew that he existed in the presence of his Echo. In a baby's earliest stages of development, before he knows that he is a separate entity from his mother or parent, he needs to be experienced and mirrored back to know that he exists. A mother who plays with her baby, imitating his goo-goos and imitating his facial expressions, assures him that he exists. For babies who did not have this need met by their parents, the need to be mirrored is a driving force in choosing a relationship. This can be a healthy need or it can become an all-consuming project full of manipulations and control maneuvers. The major difference is the level of emotional compulsion; if you feel that you are not a whole person, the need to fuse to become whole regulates your life, hence, a failure of mirroring is a failure to validate that you exist. If however, you see this need for an echo as healthy narcissism, you can tolerate failures of mirroring.

Choosing by Psychological Need

There is nothing abnormal about choosing a mate based on your own psychological needs. Healthy couples do it. A very messy person may need a person to instill a little order in his life, just as a very serious person may need someone light-hearted to shed some sunshine. Where this becomes a problem is in relationships where the need is unconscious.

A woman who likes to play the savior may gravitate towards men she can rescue. This actually serves her well if she likes to be in control. The negative part of this was pointed out by both Claude Steiner in his definition of the rescue triangle in *Games Alcoholics Play* and also by Robin Norwood in *Women Who Love Too Much*. Rescuing works fine as long as the man doesn't grow. However, if he grows and obtains any self-esteem during the relationship, he often turns around and persecutes you because the message you really are sending him is that he is incapable of doing x, y, or z by himself. As Norwood pointed out, rescuing also serves to keep women unfulfilled, because eventually the men they choose get better and leave them.

Kate, 36, grew up in an emotionally distant family. She worshipped her father, who was an alcoholic and thus emotionally unavailable to her. She and her mother fought constantly. Her mother wanted to live vicariously through Kate, and Kate withdrew, becoming remote as a way of handling her mother's invasive intensity.

She met John, 38, whose father had died, and whose mother was over-involved with him. To substitute for the emptiness in her own life, Kate pursued John, which only caused him to withdraw. He experienced her as overly close and overly demanding. So she pursued John and John retreated. It wasn't until she understood that she was repeating the same pattern she had developed with her mother that she was able to stop chasing emotionally unavailable men.

CHAPTER FOUR

Choosing With Your Brains
Instead of Your Hormones

*U*sing your brains instead of your hormones means looking beyond the chemical attraction, or the unconscious psychological need for completion, to the characteristics that will make a relationship nurture you and endure. The key is to figure out what you need in a mate, and not to waste too much time on candidates who don't have the qualifications you are seeking.

Think of dating as if you were interviewing candidates for the job of life partner. If you were planning to hire an employee, you wouldn't just hire the first person to apply. You would analyze what the job entailed, then draw up a list of skills and experience that applicants ought to have. You'd draw up a list of criteria you needed in an employee, then you would screen as many candidates as necessary to find someone who was qualified for the job and who you thought to be dependable and reliable. If, after a short period, the person you hired wasn't working out, you would fire him or her and look for a replacement. You wouldn't just continue to pay the person, hoping that eventually he or she would get better.

Yet many women do not consider what criteria they are looking for in a mate, and just date any man who asks them. If the men continue to ask them out, they keep accepting, and drift into a relationship. Even if they can see that it isn't going to work out, they cling to the relationship, hoping that the man will change or that things will get better.

Nobody is perfect, and you aren't going to find someone who fulfills all of your wants and needs. It is unrealistic to expect that you will get 100 percent of what you want. But you deserve to have 70 to 80 percent of your needs met and you shouldn't settle for less than 50 percent. The biggest mistake you can make is to stay too long in a relationship with someone who isn't right for you, hoping that magically he will change.

What You See is What You Get

One of the most common mistakes people make is thinking they can change their mates. There are certain things some people are willing to change, like how much they exercise and what kinds of foods they are willing to eat. Some people may be willing to give up drugs, alcohol, or cigarettes, but if the person isn't really willing to make these changes, he or she will become resentful of the partner making the demands. Sometimes one partner will gain weight on purpose, or smoke even more, to assert their right to make their own choices.

If you don't like a man the way he is when you meet him, don't expect that he is going to change. Accept him the way he is or move on. All personality characteristics have their down side. If you are attracted to a man because he is kind and sweet, don't expect him to be an aggressive businessman. If you are attracted to a man because he's so macho and domineering, you'd better be prepared for him to want to have his own way. Having expectations that contradict the personality characteristics of your mate will lead you into many problems.

Decide What You Want

What are you looking for in a mate? What kind of occupation do you want him to have? Does his race, religion, or political party matter to you? Is it important to you to continue to live in the same city where you live now, or are you willing to move? Do you want a man who puts his job first, or do you want a partner who places family life above all?

There are no right or wrong answers to these questions. What is right for one woman is wrong for the next, so you have to decide for yourself what qualities are important to you. One way to start is to think about what was wrong with the last man with whom you had a relationship. What qualities did he lack? These are probably some of the qualities that you are looking for in a man.

Exercise:

Make a list of the qualities that you liked in your last boyfriend, or in the relationship that lasted the longest, and what qualities you thought he was lacking.

Evaluate Your Last Boyfriend	
What did you like?	**What was missing?**

Strengths That Make Marriages Work

While most people are first attracted to a potential mate by their looks or by "chemistry," five areas seem to be most important in determining if a relationship will last. These are: compatible personality traits; shared values, accomplishments and pastimes; and relationship skills.

You can begin to reflect on these factors by thinking about the questions below. If you like, take a sheet of paper and jot down some notes. Writing may help you reflect and remember.

1. What personality traits do you want in a mate?
2. How well do the two of you communicate?
3. How do you and your potential spouse handle conflict?
4. How important to you is his income? How will money be handled?
5. Do you share leisure time interests?
6. How sexually compatible are you?
7. Do you both want to have children? (Or do neither of you want more children?)
8. Do you agree about the role of family and friends?
9. Do you agree about role expectations?
10. Do you share religious values?
11. Do you both share the same definition of what it means to be close?
12. Do you have the same degree of flexibility or is one of you more rigid?
13. Do you see the world the same way?

The most important areas in which to be compatible are values, personality traits, level of desired intimacy, expected roles, and sexuality.

What to Look for In Mr. Right

Compatibility

Personality traits

Level of desired intimacy

Sexuality (frequency & acceptable practices)

Life Stage

Similar role expectations

Shared Values

Religion

Money

Politics

Importance of Family & Friends

Similar role expectations

Accomplishment & Pastimes

Education

Career

Finances

Hobbies

Relationship Skills

Good Verbal Communication

Problem solving abilities

Good sexual communication

Personality Traits

Personality traits are enduring characteristics of a person which are subject to little change over a lifetime. Psychologists used to believe that traits were the result of how a person was nurtured, but now there is a belief that some traits may be genetic.

In thinking about choosing a mate, you need to consider what traits you like, what traits you can tolerate in another person, and

The Wedding Cake Process of Filtering Potential Mates

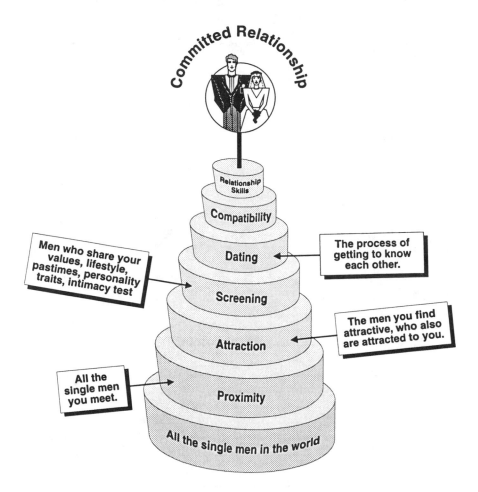

what traits are offensive to you. Personality traits include optimism, pessimism, extroversion and introversion, adaptability, adventurousness, dependability, and pragmatism.

Exercise:

On the following list, rate the traits you see in yourself and the traits you think you would like in a mate. When you have marked all the traits, go back and prioritize them, choosing the five most important traits you would like in a life partner and the three which are the most repugnant to you.

Personality Trait Matcher

Here are some qualities that you might find in a man. Rate yourself, on a scale of 1 to 5, on these qualities, and then put down on a scale of 1 to 5 how important you think these qualities would be in a mate.

Trait	You	Potential Mate
Adventurous	①②③④⑤	①②③④⑤
Affectionate	①②③④⑤	①②③④⑤
Affluent	①②③④⑤	①②③④⑤
Aggressive	①②③④⑤	①②③④⑤
Altruistic	①②③④⑤	①②③④⑤
Bold	①②③④⑤	①②③④⑤
Boyish	①②③④⑤	①②③④⑤
Calm	①②③④⑤	①②③④⑤
Carefree	①②③④⑤	①②③④⑤
Charming	①②③④⑤	①②③④⑤
Clever	①②③④⑤	①②③④⑤
Compromising	①②③④⑤	①②③④⑤
Considerate	①②③④⑤	①②③④⑤
Conventional	①②③④⑤	①②③④⑤
Courageous	①②③④⑤	①②③④⑤
Cute	①②③④⑤	①②③④⑤
Dependable	①②③④⑤	①②③④⑤
Dynamic	①②③④⑤	①②③④⑤
Emotional	①②③④⑤	①②③④⑤
Empathetic	①②③④⑤	①②③④⑤
Excitable	①②③④⑤	①②③④⑤
Extravagant	①②③④⑤	①②③④⑤
Extroverted	①②③④⑤	①②③④⑤
Family-oriented	①②③④⑤	①②③④⑤
Flexible	①②③④⑤	①②③④⑤
Forceful	①②③④⑤	①②③④⑤
Friend-oriented	①②③④⑤	①②③④⑤
Friendly	①②③④⑤	①②③④⑤
Funny	①②③④⑤	①②③④⑤
Good listener	①②③④⑤	①②③④⑤
Handsome	①②③④⑤	①②③④⑤
Happy-go-lucky	①②③④⑤	①②③④⑤
Honest	①②③④⑤	①②③④⑤
Humanitarian	①②③④⑤	①②③④⑤
Humble	①②③④⑤	①②③④⑤
Idealistic	①②③④⑤	①②③④⑤
Impulsive	①②③④⑤	①②③④⑤
Intelligent	①②③④⑤	①②③④⑤

Trait	You	Potential Mate
Introverted	①②③④⑤	①②③④⑤
Inventive	①②③④⑤	①②③④⑤
Lighthearted	①②③④⑤	①②③④⑤
Loving	①②③④⑤	①②③④⑤
Loyal	①②③④⑤	①②③④⑤
Macho	①②③④⑤	①②③④⑤
Mannerly	①②③④⑤	①②③④⑤
Mellow	①②③④⑤	①②③④⑤
Methodical	①②③④⑤	①②③④⑤
Modest	①②③④⑤	①②③④⑤
Moralistic	①②③④⑤	①②③④⑤
Open-minded	①②③④⑤	①②③④⑤
Optimistic	①②③④⑤	①②③④⑤
Philosophical	①②③④⑤	①②③④⑤
Polished	①②③④⑤	①②③④⑤
Pragmatic	①②③④⑤	①②③④⑤
Prominent	①②③④⑤	①②③④⑤
Provocative	①②③④⑤	①②③④⑤
Prudent	①②③④⑤	①②③④⑤
Quick	①②③④⑤	①②③④⑤
Religious	①②③④⑤	①②③④⑤
Reserved	①②③④⑤	①②③④⑤
Resilient	①②③④⑤	①②③④⑤
Risk taker	①②③④⑤	①②③④⑤
Romantic	①②③④⑤	①②③④⑤
Rugged	①②③④⑤	①②③④⑤
Self-sacrificing	①②③④⑤	①②③④⑤
Sense of humor	①②③④⑤	①②③④⑤
Sensitive	①②③④⑤	①②③④⑤
Sexy	①②③④⑤	①②③④⑤
Shy	①②③④⑤	①②③④⑤
Smart	①②③④⑤	①②③④⑤
Sophisticated	①②③④⑤	①②③④⑤
Stimulating	①②③④⑤	①②③④⑤
Subtle	①②③④⑤	①②③④⑤
Sweet	①②③④⑤	①②③④⑤
Sympathetic	①②③④⑤	①②③④⑤
Talkative	①②③④⑤	①②③④⑤
Tender	①②③④⑤	①②③④⑤
Traditional	①②③④⑤	①②③④⑤
Unassuming	①②③④⑤	①②③④⑤
Understanding	①②③④⑤	①②③④⑤
Unpretentious	①②③④⑤	①②③④⑤
Warm	①②③④⑤	①②③④⑤
Witty	①②③④⑤	①②③④⑤

Personality Types

Another way of thinking about personality characteristics is to lump them into large categories called types. Carl G. Jung divided personality traits into polarities; if a person had a dominant trait such as thinking, an opposite, recessive part of the polarity, feeling, was experienced more unconsciously. In each of four categories, people express a dominant characteristic and repress its opposite. Jung felt that the major goal of the second half of life was the integration of the repressed parts of yourself.

People are often very drawn to someone who is their exact opposite. However, they frequently find living with that person day-in-and-day-out very difficult because the person is so different. If you are extremely neat and organized, it may drive you crazy to live with a sloppy, disorganized person. On the other hand, you may enjoy keeping things tidy for both of you. If you are the messy one, maybe you feel you need to have someone to keep you organized and to be efficient for you. If you are an introvert, you may be drawn to an extrovert, and feel that he opens you up and broadens your horizons. But if you live with an extrovert, you will have to learn to make compromises about going out and doing things perhaps more often than you feel comfortable, because he will have more of a need to be around people than you do. Often people are attracted to someone who is different from them as a way of growing, but it can be very frustrating as well.

A relationship with someone very different from you can be exciting, but it also requires good relationship skills, such as communicating, negotiating and compromising. Differences which at first are attractive can become annoying with time. On the other hand, the problem with choosing someone too similar to you is that it can become boring. Living with the person can feel like living with yourself and lack stimulation. The best choice is a person who is like you in some ways and different from you in other ways.

"I tell people that it depends on how much they are willing to grow," says Judith Stevens-Long, Ph.D., a professor of psychology at the University of Washington, Tacoma. She has lectured and written about how to use personality types as a way of choosing friends, lovers, and employees, and as a way of better understanding other people.

"If you are interested in learning a lot about yourself and about someone else, it is a good thing to choose someone different, but you also have to be patient and tolerant, and value the differences in the other person. If you just want a nice, comfortable, easy relationship, kind of a backbone relationship, then you should choose someone more like yourself," she says.

If two people are too similar, they may need to rely on other people to balance what they lack. If two very messy and disorganized people choose each other, they may, for example, be more successful in their personal relationship if they hire housekeepers and tax accountants to keep their personal affairs organized for them.

Jung theorized that differences in behavior were a result of basic personality preferences formulated early in life. His 1923 *Psychological Types* outlined the classifications, and during the 1930s, a woman named Katharine Briggs and her daughter, Isabel Briggs Myers, worked out a questionnaire to determine personality types, called the Myers-Briggs Type Indicator.

According to this theory, there are four pairs of dominant personality types. Within each pair of characteristics there is one that you prefer.

If your dominant type is...	Your recessive type is...
Extroverted	Introverted
Sensing	Intuitive
Thinking	Feeling
Judging	Perceiving

Altogether there are 16 different personality modes, mixing and matching the four dominant traits, but you can be very introverted or slightly introverted, very sensing or slightly sensing. That means that a person who is very introverted is more opposite from someone who is very extroverted than two people who are both nearer the middle of the scale. (Just because a person's dominant mode is thinking, does not mean that he does not have feelings, of course. And a feeling person is capable of looking at things intellectually.)

You don't have to take the Myers-Briggs test to be able to figure out what mode you are most comfortable in. Remember, people are usually attracted to their own undeveloped side and Jung's theory was that you shift in the second half of life to experience your recessive traits.

Extroverts

Extroverts are people who draw energy from being with other people. This doesn't mean that they aren't good at doing things that require them to be solitary. An extrovert can be a good student and can spend hours working alone. But while the extrovert is alone, he is draining the charge on his internal battery. He needs to be with people to recharge himself emotionally. Extroverts are frequently talkative, gregarious people who are approachable and are able to talk to strangers easily. Usually they like parties and large gatherings and prefer generating ideas with a group. Extroverts take in energy from other people. An extrovert may be tired before going to a party, but once he gets there and starts talking to people, he is energized, revved up. He feels better as the evening goes along.

Introverts

Introverts need to be alone to re-charge themselves. They enjoy peace and quiet and being alone, and prefer one-on-one conversations to large gatherings. This doesn't mean that an introvert can't be successful in social situations or can't do a job well that requires a lot of human contact. But the tip-off is that the introvert is likely to find dealing with a lot of people exhausting, and needs to regather strength by being alone for awhile. Sometimes introverts are considered shy, and may come across as being quiet and reserved. Introverts typically have very intense relationships and are less easy-going than extroverts.

Sensing Types

Sensing type people like things to be concrete and tangible. They usually understand the ins and outs of a situation, know the short-cuts and where to get the best bargains, and know who the person is you have to see if you want to get something done. They like facts and figures instead of theories, they do things in order, and like to have clear instructions. By definition, sensing types are tuned into their senses, into how things look, smell, feel, and taste.

Intuitive Types

Intuitive people are the kind of people who say, "I can't explain why, I just know." They may be considered absent-minded or be called space cadets. They see the possibilities in a situation, and they aren't very interested in details. Extroverted intuitive types recognize trends before they start. Successful businessmen and women frequently rely on their intuition to make choices.

Thinking Types

Thinkers deal with issues intellectually, instead of emotionally. They are cool and objective, and try to be fair. They think it is more important to be right than well-liked, and they don't mind making difficult decisions.

Feeling Types

Feeling types think with their hearts. They are concerned with feelings and emotions, and try to put themselves into the shoes of others. They like to take care of other people, and will go out of their way to be helpful. They are often accused of wearing their hearts on their sleeve, or of taking things too personally.

Judging Types

People who are judging types are very orderly and organized. They believe that there is a place for everything, and everything should be in its place.   They make lists and schedules and they stick to them.   The judger is the kind of person who plans the entire itinerary for a trip, makes hotel reservations in advance, and always has a rent-a-car waiting.   He likes to work things through to completion and have them out of the way.

Perceiving Types

A perceiver is a flexible person.   He is less likely to plan, and is more spontaneous.   He is likely to go on a vacation without reservations, and to cope with whatever situation he finds when he gets there.   He works in last-minute spurts of energy to meet deadlines, and is more concerned with creativity and spontaneity than neatness or organization.

Balancing Opposite Types

David Keirsey and Marilyn Bates, in their book *Please Understand Me*, and Otto Kroeger and Janet M. Thuesen, in their book *Type Talk*, list all sixteen personality types with a thumbnail sketch of each.   Both of these books give a more comprehensive discussion of all sixteen personality modes and how they interact.

Very frequently introverts are attracted to extroverts, because the extrovert can talk easily and can keep the conversation going.   The introvert may feel that the extroverted one will carry the ball socially and help him or her get out into the world more.   The extrovert may appreciate the fact that the introvert lets him or her do a lot of the talking, and bask in the spotlight.   The introvert enjoys listening and not having to carry the conversation himself.   If both parties enjoy the other one's differentness, and if they can accommodate the other's needs, this opposition can work well. Where it gets into trouble is when the introverted person decides that the extroverted one wants to go out too much, that he or she is never content just to stay home, and where the extroverted one feels that the introverted one is boring and a stick-in-the-mud because he or she never wants to go anywhere.   Both sides need to accommodate the other so that the introvert gets to spend enough time alone and the extrovert gets to spend enough time out with other people.

Two introverts may find that a perfect evening is staying home together watching television, while two extroverts think the perfect evening is going to a rock concert and then to a crowded restaurant.

Thinkers and Feelers

Because standard sex roles condition men to be dominant thinking types and women to be feeling types, it is likely that you will find someone who is opposite you in this category. Thinkers do have feelings, of course, but they need to come to grips with them intellectually before they can articulate them.

Dan was a Thinker and Dick was a Feeler. When Dick's girlfriend was upset about something, Dick instinctively held her, patted her, and said things like, "I guess you're feeling bad. Don't worry, everything's going to be all right." He automatically understood what to do to show her that he cared about her feelings.

In similar situations, Dan seemed perplexed. He asked questions and tried to understand what the problem was. A few hours later, or the next day, he sympathized with his girlfriend in almost the same way that Dick had. The difference was that before Dan could be sympathetic and supportive, he had to think about what the problem was and analyze what the right response would be. He could be emotionally supportive once he figured out that was what was called for, while Dick was intuitively empathetic.

Judgers and Perceivers

Since judgers are typically very neat and orderly and perceivers disorganized and spontaneous, this is an area where people who are initially attracted by their differences can grow to be very annoyed by them. Marcia, 36, a nursery school teacher, was dominantly perceiving, and she was initially attracted to Lew, 37, an accountant, because he was so good at organizing and taking care of things. She loved having him take care of paying the bills and seeing to it that her car was always filled with gas. But she became annoyed when he criticized her disorganized cabinets and messy filing system. Marcia's spontaneity delighted Lew in the beginning, but he found it annoying to get up in the morning and discover there was no milk in the refrigerator to pour over his breakfast cereal.

The Attraction of Opposites

A popular romantic notion is that opposites attract. And it's true; they do. The attraction of opposites fits into the completion fantasy which is part of the theme of romantic love. But there are dangers in looking for completion.

Joann and Peter were as different as any two people could be. She was from a stable, close-knit family and was a very optimistic, upbeat person. Peter's parents were divorced, and he had a very difficult adjustment when his mother remarried. Peter was a born pessimist. In the beginning, Joann was constantly amazed at what a bleak picture Peter portrayed, and he always saw her optimism as unfounded.

After the birth of their two children, their problems mounted. Instead of sharing with each other, they became increasingly silent. Peter missed the companionship most because he had few other close friends; Joann, on the other hand, confided in her sister and her co-workers.   She had stopped talking to Peter, because she hated for him to rain on her parade.   It didn't matter what she wanted to talk about, he usually foresaw the worst possible scenario.   Joann had decided that it was better to keep silent than to be squelched by his negative thoughts.

Although both Joann and Peter were devoted to their children, they felt the difference in their personality traits to be too great to surmount. The way Peter responded to Joann had shut her down for so long, she no longer felt attracted to him. The result was that Joann and Peter got divorced.

Charles and Maggie were also opposites.   She was a bubbly extrovert who worked as an area consultant for a major cosmetics firm.   She loved talking to people at work, and socializing after hours.   She could go out seven nights a week and still not feel burned out.   Her husband, on the other hand, was a quiet, very serious attorney.   When Charles met Maggie, he was attracted to her effervescence, and thought she could help him become more socially adept.   He also assumed that Maggie would be less extroverted when she settled down into marriage.

What Charles and Maggie had in common was their mutual respect and their closeness to family and friends.   In the beginning, they seemed very happy together.   But after three years of marriage, Maggie was bored staying home, and Charles was irritated when she went out without him.   He interpreted her socializing as a rejection of him, meaning that other people were more important to her than he was.   She nagged him to go out with her more often, and he accused her of being frivolous and superficial because she didn't enjoy staying at home night after night.   The issue of Charles' introversion and Maggie's extroversion was a problem, with each trying to change the other or suggesting that the other was wrong.

With help, they came to understand that extroversion and introversion are character traits, not moral issues.   Neither was wrong in how they behaved, but if they wanted the relationship to endure, each of them needed to compromise.   They stopped blaming each other and accepted the other as different and looked for ways to accommodate each other's needs.   Charles agreed to go out with Maggie on Friday and Saturday nights, and agreed not to complain when she went out with girlfriends two evenings a week. She agreed to stay home with him on the other evenings.   Their sex life improved immediately and the marriage endured.

Level of Desired Intimacy

How close do you like to be to another person? Is your idea of a perfect relationship one in which the couple does everything together? Do you want to spend all of your evenings and all of your weekends together, or are you more comfortable spending some time together and some time apart with other friends?

For example, would you be comfortable if your husband played cards with the guys every Thursday night, played golf with the fellows on Sundays, and visited his parents without you? Would you be comfortable taking separate vacations?

There is a wide range of styles of intimacy ranging from very close to disengaged. If you select someone who is very different from you, in terms of the level of closeness desired, you will probably be very unhappy. In fact, sometimes comfort with different levels of intimacy leads to feelings of jealousy or abandonment.

Exercise:

One way to assess how intimate you like to be would be to complete the following statements:

1. On the weekends, I would like to be together...
   - ① ...all the time
   - ② ...most of the time
   - ③ ...some of the time
   - ④ ...infrequently
   - ⑤ ...almost never

2. I want to eat dinner together...
   - ① ...all the time
   - ② ...most of the time
   - ③ ...some of the time
   - ④ ...infrequently
   - ⑤ ...almost never

3. I'm comfortable with my partner spending time with friends of his or her same sex...
   - ⑤ ...once a week
   - ④ ...once or twice a month
   - ③ ...a few times a year
   - ② ...once a year
   - ① ...never

4. When visiting my family, I want my partner to come with me
   - ① ...once a week
   - ② ...once or twice a month
   - ③ ...a few times a year
   - ④ ...once a year
   - ⑤ ...never

5. When my partner's children are with us for the weekend, I'm comfortable with him spending time with them alone without me

    ⑤ ...all weekend
    ④ ...one day of the weekend
    ③ ...one night of the weekend
    ② ...an occasional trip or event (once or twice a year)
    ① ...not at all

6. I would feel comfortable taking vacations

    ⑤ ...once or twice a year without my mate
    ③ ...once every few years without my mate
    ① ...never without my mate

To figure out your score, add up the numbers you gave yourself and divide them by six. If your score is one or two, you want a high degree of togetherness. If your score is three you are comfortable both being close and being separate. If your score is four or five you are comfortable being separate much of the time.

Compatible mates usually either share the same level of desired intimacy or else are adaptable enough to tolerate what their partner needs. But that requires careful communication, mutual respect, and a bit of work.

Birth Order

Another way in which people pair up is in terms of birth order. Birth order affects the role one learned to play. For instance, frequently the eldest brother or sister inherits a caretaker role. They are asked to look out after their younger siblings and if they fail to do this they are punished. Eldest children may need to seek out others when they have problems because they were more indulged and attended to as children.

However, oldest children frequently marry a youngest child who is accustomed to being taken care of. These roles aren't prescribed by birth order, but there are some who believe strongly in their viability. Nancy, 29, the youngest of three, has been married to Larry, 39, also the youngest of three, for ten years. She complained, "We both want to be taken care of." She was aware of the birth order position and the effect it had on their marriage.

"I'm tired of being the one to do all the taking care of," she said referring to her role as mother not only to her three children, but also to her husband.

Sexual Desire

When couples are sexually compatible, sex is only part of a good relationship, but when the sexual relationship is poor, it becomes all-important. Sexual relations fulfill a biological urge, but they also become the stage on which a relationship's problems are acted out. The basic problems couples have stem from different levels of desire, and different tolerances of accepted practices. Since sex becomes a symbol of the relationship, sexual dissatisfaction usually creates a serious problem.

It is unlikely that a couple will be happy together if their level of sexual desire is very different. Generally, it is the person who wants sex least who should control the frequency because feeling pressured turns him or her off even more. If one partner wants to have sex twice a week and the other wants to have it once a month, expect on-going conflicts.

According to a 1986 Masters, Johnson, & Kolodny study, the average American married couple reports having sexual intercourse two or three times a week through young adulthood, tapering off to about once a week after the age of fifty. However, there are wide individual differences. The important thing is that if one partner wants to have sex once a month, he will not be compatible with a partner who wishes to have relations every day.

It is also important to feel comfortable with your partner's preferred sexual practices and degree of diversity. Partners should feel equally comfortable with most of the sexual practices employed.

A major problem is that some people use sex for validation, as their only way of being close. A man may like to have sex just as a form of physical release, while his partner may want to have sexual relationships only within an intimate context, insisting on extensive foreplay.

Life Stage

Everybody starts out single. When you marry for the first time, you probably expect to live happily ever after, but it is not uncommon to find yourself single again later in life, due to divorce or the death of a partner. The experience of being single varies tremendously from one stage of life to another. Being single at 20 is very different than being single at 40. At 20, most people have not yet found a mate. At 40, singles include never married women and men, as well as divorced or widowed men and women, some of whom hope to remarry someday. (Eighty percent of divorced men and 75 percent of divorced women eventually remarry.)

A 38-year-old career woman who has never married is likely to be looking for something different in a marriage partner than a 38-year-old divorced mother of two, who has just gotten a job after getting divorced. A woman who is still interested in having children has different needs in a mate than a woman who has already had her children.

Likewise, a 38-year-old man who has never married and has no children probably has different needs from a 38-year-old father of three who has joint physical custody of his children, trading them back and forth with his ex-wife on alternate weeks. Life stage issues complicate the choice of a mate.

Knowing What You're Ready For

Julia was widowed at 53, and wanted to be with a man who was still working. It took her two years to meet him, but Mr. Right showed up, along with two not-yet-grown children. At 55, with her own children grown, Julia wasn't eager to take on the role of stepmother, but she was flexible enough to see that Herb offered her more of what she wanted in a man than what she didn't want. She realized that sometimes we can't have 100 percent of what we want in life, and she decided to be content with 85 percent.

It was a different story for Candy, a 48-year-old divorcee with two teenaged children. When Candy met Tom at a singles dance, they hit it off immediately. Candy and her ex-husband had traveled extensively, and she had continued her world travels as a single woman, sometimes taking her children, sometimes going with a woman friend, and sometimes joining an organized tour. She loved to travel, and to talk about her travels, and to hear other people talk about where they had been. When thinking about what she wanted in a man, Candy had realized that she wanted a man who liked to travel as much as she did, who had the time to travel with her, and who could afford the kind of foreign travel she enjoyed.

When Tom introduced himself to Candy and another woman as they stood chatting at a singles dance, Candy detected a foreign accent and asked him where he was from.

"Hungary, originally," he replied, "But I've been in the United States for 30 years."

"Oh really? I love Budapest," Candy replied.

"You've been to Budapest?" Tom asked in surprise. "When?"

"Last summer, and six years ago," Candy said. "Have you been back since you left?"

"Oh, yes, I go every year," Tom said. "I guess you must like to travel."

"It's my major passion," Candy said, and Tom said, "Mine too," as the woman who had been talking to Candy drifted away.

After another 45 minutes of animated conversation, Tom asked Candy for her telephone number. The next night he called to invite her to dinner. The first date was fun, and they realized that they had a number of other interests in common, and many shared values.

However, Tom was 65 years old, and ready to retire. He was healthy and energetic, and affluent enough to share the kind of lifestyle Candy enjoyed. But he had also been planning for years to spend his retirement in nearly constant travel. He owned a recreational vehicle, and hoped to take it for trips several months in duration around the United States and Canada, and to spend three and four months at a time in foreign travels.

It was a lifestyle that Candy knew would appeal to her if she were older and at a different stage in her life. But she was still immersed in her career, her teaching job prevented her from traveling except during the summer, and she had two children who were still at home. Although Tom and Candy were attracted to each other, after dating for several months, they realized that they were not a good match, because they were at different stages in their life cycles. Candy didn't think it was fair to ask Tom to sit twiddling his thumbs while she worked, giving up his lifelong dream of travel. If Candy had been 10 years older, they might have been a perfect match.

Sharing a Sense of Humor

You don't have to ask a man any questions to determine whether or not he has a good sense of humor; you observe it. If he cracks silly jokes and you don't think he is serious enough, chances are you won't find his jokes any funnier the tenth or hundredth time you hear them.

Do you laugh at the same things? Does he make you laugh? Do you make him laugh? Do you find the same scenes in movies funny, or sad, or touching? If you can laugh with each other, it is easier to get over some of the hurdles which living together can present. Humor can be a powerful means of resolving conflicts as well as getting through rough times.

Sharing Values

Most people tend to feel most comfortable with others who share similar values. Values are frequently unconsciously accepted, and whereas people can adapt to different pastimes, different values tend to grate on people's nerves. For example, if you are close to your family and value their input, and you marry a man who is just the opposite, he may resent your snoopy mother and refuse to accompany you to family events.

The kinds of questions you can ask to begin to understand and compare values include:

1. How much time do you like to spend with your family?
2. What role do friends play in your life?

3. What roles should men and women play?
4. What are your religious or political beliefs?

Values separate people.   People with similar values are your friends and people with dissimilar values are your associates. Values have to do with how you see the world and what responsibility you feel you have in terms of it.   Values include religious beliefs, political beliefs, the importance of honesty or truthfulness, and traditional versus non-traditional role expectations.

Religion

Some couples are very happy together despite obvious differences in religious or political beliefs.   Sometimes the belief system is strongly held by one person and the second person is more indifferent.   Sometimes both hold belief systems with equal vigor, but they have so much respect for each other that they are able to tolerate the differences; they make no effort to change the other person.   Another combination is couples who belong to different churches, but who place equal value on the importance of religious beliefs.   But some couples do split up over religious differences.

Jane was a non-practicing Jew while Jonathan was a practicing Christian.   He was willing to let her bring up the children in her faith, but he insisted that they be brought up with some faith.   She wasn't comfortable with this and their different values became a point of contention. Eventually they separated and both found new partners who shared their religious values.

Religious differences can be overcome, but they can also function as a source of conflict in many couples, particularly around the holidays.   If they can reach an agreeable compromise, it can work out, but if one member is unwilling to compromise, it can create a problem.

Sandy is Episcopalian and Jeffrey is Jewish.   She was comfortable trying to celebrate his holidays such as lighting the Sabbath candles, but she was very hurt when on Christmas Eve she asked him to go to her church and he refused.

Sometimes it does not seem on the surface as though there will be a direct religious conflict, but the difference in the degree of religiosity can cause friction in daily life.   If both partners are Protestants, for example, but one comes from a family that holds hands and prays at every meal, and the other from a family where the observation of Christianity is limited to buying a Christmas tree and coloring eggs on Easter, this may lead to conflicts.

Abigail was brought up as a Protestant, but has not practiced any religion as an adult, and considers herself to be non-religious. Donald was delighted to hear that when he met her, because he is vociferously opposed to organized religion. Most of the women he met, he told her, were too pious and he was happy to meet an intelligent woman who shared his point of view. Unfortunately, Donald felt so strongly about his anti-religious feelings that he wanted to discuss them all the time. It was his favorite topic, and Abigail was as uninterested in hearing what was wrong with religion as she was in hearing what was good about it. She stopped seeing Donald because she hated to hear him talk about his dislike of religion all the time.

She married Stephen, who had been raised in a Jewish household, but who hadn't practiced any religion as an adult. Abigail and Stephen had no religious conflicts at all. They both had basic Judeo-Christian values, and neither of them practiced any religious ritual in everyday life. They celebrated Christmas in a non-religious way, and ignored all other religious holidays. Having been raised with different faiths caused them no problems whatsoever.

Roles

A new area of conflict for couples is what roles men and women are expected to play. A man who grew up in a household where Mother was waiting after school with cookies and milk and always had Dad's dinner on the table, is likely to assume that his wife will take on the same roles, even if she works outside the home.

For couples who wish to be traditional, the role relationships are fairly clear-cut. But for many couples caught in changing trends, the expectations need to be defined, which can be frustrating, confusing, and a source of conflict.

Exercise:

Some questions to consider which will give you a fairly clear description of role expectations are:
1. Who is responsible for raising children or is this a jointly held role?
2. When there is an emergency with the children, are both parties equally able to fill in or is it one person's role more than the other?
3. Who will be responsible for overseeing the household chores, if not doing them?
4. In your parents' household, and in the household of your prospective spouses' parents, who played what roles? Do you want to duplicate these roles?
5. If your prospective spouse is divorced, who played what roles in his previous marriage?

Finding a Balance

Joe, a 30-year-old businessman, worked very hard and was fairly successful. Jill had just finished law school and was beginning work as an attorney. Their lives went very smoothly until they had children. They constantly fought over who would stay home when the baby was sick. Jill felt that Joe wasn't valuing her work when he insisted that she stay home. Then there were nights when the baby needed to be rocked. Jill resented that Joe felt it was her job.

Jill and Joe went for marriage counseling and worked out a compromise. He consented to increase the amount of time he spent with the children and to take on a few more chores at home, and they agreed to hire a housekeeper at least one day a week. They also realized that they had spent so little time together as a couple that their intimacy and their sex life had suffered, and they agreed to rectify that by getting a babysitter so they could go out more often together.

Research has shown that mothers who work are happiest when the father is at least minimally involved either in childcare or housework. (The average father puts in 1.8 hours of work in these areas per day, while the average working wife devotes 4.8 hours per day.) The one area where men are willing to devote more time is toward their children. Marriages that have involved fathers report greater satisfaction than families in which the father is married to his career, with his family and wife coming second and third.

Money

Money and how we handle it has a lot to do with how we feel about power. Some people are very generous with their money and others guard it carefully. Since money matters are one of the greatest sources of conflict between couples (it ties with sexual dissatisfaction as a reason why couples come in for counseling), how people feel about money and how they use it are issues to be discussed. Particularly in later marriages where both parties work and have accumulated properties, how these matters are going to be handled needs to be worked out.

Exercise:

1. Do you think you will want a prenuptial agreement?
2. How do you envision handling money?
3. Will you combine your resources or keep them separate?
4. Will you reach joint decisions on major expenses or do all expenditures need to be discussed?
5. Will you have a joint checking account or separate accounts?
6. Who will pay the household bills?
7. Do you need to tell each other how much money you have?

8. Who has more power in the relationship? Is it held equally? Does it attach to the larger wage earner? Is it split along traditional lines where the man has control over large expenses and the wife has control over the household and the children?

9. How do you feel about this division of power?

Commitment to Family and Friends

Observing how a person maintains (or doesn't maintain) his friendships is a good indicator of personality and values. How does he get along with his own relatives? Are there relatives with whom he is no longer associated? If so, what caused the rift in the relationship? You can learn a lot about people by their personal associations, because how he or she has treated old friends, acquaintances, and family members in the past is likely how he or she will treat you. The exception might be if the person has done a significant amount of psychological work to change how he was in a past relationship.

If the man is divorced and has children, what kind of relationship does he maintain with his children? If there is no relationship with children, why isn't there one?

Sometimes in step-family situations newly married women feel threatened by the new husband's relationship with his children, and, through them, his need to maintain contact with his ex-wife. There are ongoing questions to work out about custody and visitation periods, as well as decisions about education and medical care. These relationships are emotionally loaded, and too often the children find themselves in the middle.

A useful approach is to befriend step-children, while encouraging your spouse to set up and maintain the new rules of your household. Acknowledging to the child what a difficult situation it is to have competing loyalties to two people (their parents) who aren't getting along might help the child see that he or she doesn't have to make a choice; he or she can love both parents and maybe even the new step-parent and family. Since it is very desirable for the children to have a loving relationship with both of their parents, a wise and loving new spouse will not interfere with that important relationship.

Desire for Children

Nearly 90 percent of women reproduce, although 10 percent report regretting this decision. People have babies for many reasons. You may feel a desire to carry out your line, some biological urge, some normal egoistic need to see yourself in another, and some religious sense that this is the purpose of a marriage. The worst reason for having a child is to save a failing marriage.

Nothing is as divisive as disagreeing about whether or not to have children. Ted told Leslie before they married that he didn't want children, but she secretly harbored the belief that she could get him to change his mind. A year after the wedding, when she told him she wanted to have a baby, Ted was furious. He felt deceived. Neither of them changed their minds, and they eventually separated.

Pastimes

When singles place personals ads, they frequently describe themselves in terms of their pastimes. Pastimes are what you do with your free time. Your idea of a good time might be to snuggle up and read a book, watch television, or listen to music, while someone else's idea involves more physical exertion; perhaps he wants to go jogging, go hiking, go windsurfing, or something else which tests his physical stamina. Many happy couples do not share all the same pastimes, but it is a good idea if you share at least some. One couple may enjoy eating out at restaurants and listening to classical music together, but when he plays golf on Saturdays, she works in her garden. Some people are not concerned if their partner spends most of his or her free time in separate pursuits. Other people feel it is important to share most of their leisure time.

Exercise:

Make a list of the things you like to do for recreation. Write down how often you like to do each activity. If you really enjoy skiing, but you only like to go two days a year, how important is it to you to have a mate who shares your interest in skiing? On the other hand, if all of your leisure time is taken up in activities sponsored by your church group, would it make sense to look for a partner who did not share your religious convictions? The following list includes activities that some people like to do.

By no means is this list meant to be exhaustive, but it can help you think about what you most like to do with your spare time. If you don't have any identifiable hobbies, now's a great time to start something new.

You need to decide how much time you want to spend in shared pursuits with your mate. The answer to that depends on your concept of intimacy. Do you expect to spend all your free time together, or can you spend part of your time together and part of your time separately?

Michael and Lynn both loved their jobs and spent a lot of time in work-related activities. When they were able to meet after work, they enjoyed going out to interesting ethnic restaurants. They both loved to go to see new films, although Michael liked going to the

Favorite Pastimes

Physical Activities
Baseball
Basketball
Biking
Bowling
Camping
Dancing
Diving
Fishing
Football
Gardening
Golfing
Hunting
Jogging
Martial Arts
Polo
Sailing
Shooting
Skating
Skiing
Snorkeling
Soccer
Square Dancing
Swimming
Walking
Water skiing
Whale watching
Wind surfing
Working out

Hobbies
Car mechanics
Cooking
Crafts
Electronics
Knitting
Needlepoint
Sewing
Television
Weaving
Wine-tasting
Woodworking

Artistic Pursuits
Drawing
Painting
Potting
Sculpting
Writing

Intellectual Activities
Book discussion groups
Church-related activities
Classes
Museums
Political campaigns
Volunteering in charity or political events

Shopping Activities
Antiques
Auctions
Clothes
Computer swap meets
Swap meets

Attending
Ballet & other forms of dance
Conferences
Lectures
Movies
Opera
Performing arts
Plays
Restaurants
Sports events
Symphony
Workshops

Socializing
Board games
Bridge
Charity events
Gambling
Getting together with friends...
  * at parties
  * for dinner
  * on the telephone
  * over coffee
  * with alcohol
Poker

Traveling
Bicycling
Camping
Car trips
Cruises
RVing
Tours
Train trips

Involvement with Animals
Pet shows
Zoo
Walking the dog

movies more often than Lynn. Almost every two weeks, he went to a movie by himself. Lynn, on the other hand, enjoyed rock concerts, which Michael hated. She frequently attended them with one of her girlfriends, and occasionally, maybe once every few years, she went to a music festival in another state.

Since Michael got more vacation time than Lynn, he sometimes went on trips to Europe and the Far East without her. He would go for a couple of weeks, and then Lynn would join him at the end of the trip for the last few weeks of the vacation.

For couples who expect to spend all their free time together, this would not be an acceptable arrangement. But for Michael and Lynn, it worked out well. This was a second marriage for both of them and they were both used to spending time on their own. They didn't feel deserted when the other one was busy; they got on the phone and made other arrangements for themselves. There are no rules about how much time happy couples spend together; it is a matter of preference.

Accomplishments, Career, and Education

Many women who were born after World War II, raised with the traditional values of the 1950s, still think they need to marry "richer, taller, older, and smarter." Despite the fact that many of them don't really need to marry a man for status, since they have their own status as a career person, the old adage creeps back into their consciousness.

The wisdom behind the old adage was that women had no status of their own. As late as the 1960s, Erikson was still saying that women needed to leave a space in their identity, in other words remain half-baked, and form their identity later based on their husband's identity and social role.

If you want to get married to increase your social status, or economic support, then you should marry up. If that is the case, then the education a man has received, and the income he can command, may be very important criteria for you.

For women who have careers and don't want to give them up, choosing a man based on his skills, profession, or income capabilities is certainly still an option. But another option is to combine these criteria with other characteristics you'd like to find in a mate, such as empathy, listening skills, and caretaking abilities.

Finding the Right Support

Gloria and Jim met when they were both in law school. Gloria described Jim as "very big and dominant, a bright, aggressive, very successful future lawyer and good provider, although I never really was looking so much for a provider as I was for an intelligent man. I had an innate feeling that the man was supposed to be superior, that I was supposed to be able to look up to the man."

When they each began practicing law, Gloria found it difficult to devote time both to her career and to being the perfect traditional wife. She found herself rushing home trying to get dinner on the table for a man who placed his career on a higher priority than hers, and who quickly began making more money than she did.

"I had to come home and kowtow to an even more successful, more stressed person, and try to consider his every need," she said.

The marriage ended after ten years when Jim began an affair with his secretary.

"That was what ultimately split us up, but it was a relationship that needed to end," Gloria said.

"I met Todd eight months after Jim and I separated. I consciously thought about wanting something very different. I wanted a man who wanted to get married, to have children, whose values were for a modest financial lifestyle, who wanted to spend time with the family instead of providing them with a lot of money.

"I wanted a man with no dark corners. I had always been attracted to the eccentric, dark, and dramatic man—which is how Jim was. I think I was colored by books and movies, the romantic ideas. I found out that the most romantic kind of a man is a good man, decent, faithful, and kind, who will be good to me and to his kids."

Gloria and Todd have been married for three years and are expecting their first child. "He is very different from my first husband. He is supportive, sensitive, kind, caring, nurturing... Now when I come home, sometimes I make dinner, sometimes he makes dinner, it's a much more equal proposition.

"Jim was a product of the 50s and 60s, what men and women were supposed to be... He was very successful financially. Jim would buy me a diamond bracelet for Valentine's Day. Todd puts up 200 paper hearts all over the house. That takes some sentiment, some effort. Jim just wrote a check. I'd rather have the paper hearts."

Gloria says that she and Todd share an interest in the arts, and they both like films, and the same kinds of sports—skiing and hiking. But she and Jim shared most of the same pastimes too.

"But you know," she says, "sharing the same values is more important. If I want to go to the opera, I can go with a girlfriend. If I want a fascinating dinner companion, it doesn't have to be my husband. I want a man who is as committed to home and family and children as I am."

Putting It Together

If you've been working through the exercises in this chapter you now have quite a few lists: your favorite pastimes, the qualities you think you'd like in a mate, values and attitudes that matter to you, preferred intimacy level, and perhaps more. You also know what your own goals are in terms of career, children, finances, and lifestyle. All this information goes into the balance when you weigh the appropriateness of a potential mate.

Take a few moments now to look over your lists, and run through your mental notes. Are there realizations that surprise you? New possible areas for compromise? All this information serves as background for your screening process. Think about what you want, need, and expect—and then try to distill your notes to the three most essential characteristics in a mate. Emphasize any area you like—life stage, intimacy level, pastimes, whatever—but try to zero in on the things that would realistically complement and support your needs in a relationship. These are the non-negotiables.

Now put your lists aside. Remember, no one gets 100 percent of what they are looking for. However, you should get 60 to 70 percent of what you think is important in the three to five most important facets of a relationship. For a potential partner to only measure up to 30 to 40 percent of your top five facets would probably be too low.

The First Date

Dating is the way you screen applicants for the job of spouse. On the first date, your goal is to find out if you like the guy enough to spend more time with him. Do you have similar values? This is not the same as interests—it doesn't mean do you both like to ski. It means do you share the same basic outlook on life.

Avoid putting your date on the spot. You can gain valuable information about him in the natural form of a good conversation, without interrogating him. Good topics for conversation on the first date include what kinds of things he likes to do for entertainment, his relationship to his family, and his work. Questions about his personal history, his life goals, and his religious or political beliefs should be reserved for subsequent meetings.

Good First Date Questions

Remember, these questions should lead to conversation—not an interview. Then again, take the answers as seriously as if you were interviewing job applicants for a very important position.

1. Where are you from?
2. Do you have brothers or sisters?
3. Are you close to them?
4. What are your memories about growing up and what do you think is important about growing up?
5. Why did you move here?

6. How do you like it here? Do you want to stay here your whole life?
7. What kind of job do you have?
8. How do you like it?
9. If you could be anything you wanted to be, what would it be?
10. If you were rich, what would you do with your money?
11. Who was your best friend when you were growing up? What did you like to do together? Do you know what happened to her or him?
12. Do you have a best friend now? What do you like about him or her?
13. Have you ever been married? Do you have any children?
14. What is your relationship with them?
15. What are your favorite restaurants?
16. What are your favorite movies?
17. What are your favorite books?
18. What are your favorite sports?
19. Do you like to garden?
20. Do you enjoy any handicrafts?
21. Do you like to shop?
22. What kind of art do you like?
23. Do you like the theater?
24. How do you spend holidays?
25. What kind of music do you like?
26. What are your favorite television programs?

The object of the first date is to see if you have anything in common other than a physical attraction. How do you feel with him? Is he interested in you? Is he animated when you talk?

If, after asking these questions and thinking about the man's responses, you think you have enough in common to go out on a second date, clearly you think that there is something there. It's time to explore further.

Questions for Subsequent Dates

1. What are your goals in life?
2. What are your regrets? If you had your life to do over, what would you do differently?
3. What would you like to accomplish in the future?
4. What was the most important part of growing up?
5. What do you want to be doing when you get old?
6. Do you believe in heaven or hell, or an afterlife?
7. How often and where do you like to go on vacations?
8. What do you think about abortion? (or some other current political topic. This tells you a great deal about a person's political views.)
9. What are your views on the role of women in the home, with children, in the business world?
10. Would you mind having a woman boss?

The point of asking these questions early in the relationship is to save time and prevent heartache. It is easier to find out during the first few dates that a man has attitudes that annoy you, than to be annoyed or enraged for the rest of your life. If you ask these questions pleasantly, and act truly interested in his answers, a man is not likely to feel that he is being grilled. Everyone likes to talk about themselves, and most men are flattered when you are interested in hearing about them. It is okay to tell the man about yourself too, but remember, whenever you are talking, you aren't learning anything (except how well he listens.)

The psychology of this screening procedure is that it puts you in control. One word of caution: don't think that you can talk about scary things like commitment, marriage, and kids, without some reaction. If you are like many women, as soon as a man says he is interested in kids, you go into high gear. Nothing is scarier to a man. The disclosure by women of their desire for children and a family has frequently been followed by a man's withdrawal. The best course may be to acknowledge to the man what a big change children bring, and how overwhelming that can be. This may help to ease the fear that causes some men to withdraw. For most men, freedom and the fear of containment are major psychological issues.

Relationship Skills

The skills that are important to look for in a prospective mate are verbal communication and problem solving ability. Are you and he able to express yourselves to each other? Can you tell each other about what you need, using statements that begin with "I" (not "you"), and not blaming one another? Is he able to explain his feelings to you, or does he expect you to read his mind? In other words, when he wants you to do something for him, does he ask directly for it? "I need for you to be more quiet while I'm studying," is clearer and less judgmental than, "You're too loud and you're bothering me." Likewise, when you want him to do something, you ought to be able to say, "I would like to know if you understand how I feel," rather than, "Sometimes you are very thick-skulled."

Good problem solving abilities involve being flexible and striving to come up with creative solutions. Are the two of you able to solve problems together, or is one of you always the rigid one, and the other one the adaptor?

CHAPTER FIVE

Conflicts of the Career Woman: The Yes, But Game

*"You women are liberated in all ways
except in your relationships."*

—Dinah Mellon,
Clinical Psychologist, 1972

*B*ecause women are traditionally brought up to value their relationships with others more than anything else, it has been assumed that they feel threatened by anything that threatens those relationships. Psychologists have asserted that women fear independence and success will threaten the important relationships in their lives. An example used to demonstrate this theory is that women tend to avoid speaking out for fear of appearing disagreeable; in mixed company, women will frequently keep quiet and let the men do the talking. This has been interpreted as a woman's way of avoiding any difference that might cause her to be seen as a separate person. If a woman equates autonomy with having a separate opinion, then any time she has a separate opinion, it could possibly be a threat to her relationships—and therefore to her self and her identity.

In 1968, Matina Horner, a psychologist, wrote about women's fears of success. She concluded that while men feared failure, women actually suffered anxiety over being successful because they perceived success as a threat to their relationships. As Horner explained: "The aggressive overtones of competition and success are evident in the fact that each time one person succeeds, someone else fails or is beaten. This may well be the basis of fear of success...."

Horner said that "Freud pointed out that the whole essence of femininity lies in repressing aggressiveness. A woman is threatened by success because unusual excellence in academic and intellectual areas is unconsciously equated with loss of femininity; as a result, the possibility of social rejection becomes very real."

Beth, the plastic surgeon who married the man her mother thought to be the ideal son-in-law, found her marriage foundering because her husband was threatened by her success. She was number two in her medical school class, ahead of him, and he had expected to be superior to his wife. Their marriage failed, and when Beth chose a second husband, she deliberately selected a man in another field, so that she could be successful in her own arena without competing directly with him. Her second husband is less competitive and is happy that Beth is so successful.

The anticipation of success in competitive achievement can produce extreme anxiety, not because of the actual success, but because of the imagined (and in some cases realized) loss of relationships that the success may cause. The fear is that you will face social rejection or that you will hurt someone else on the way to the top. The underlying assumption is, of course, that if someone wins, someone loses, and this is contrary to the feminine ethic of playing the caretaker.

If you accept this notion that women see themselves within webs of connecting relationships, and worry that their success would threaten these relationships, what happens to women who really do put relational issues aside to pursue their own goals? Do they have conflicts around their femininity? Do they repress their desires for connections? Or do they modify their ambition? Do these internal conflicts get enacted in their relationships and, if so, in what form? And are these issues around identity unique to women today? We are in a time of flux in which the meaning and roles attached to being a woman and a man are changing, and what might be true for women now might not be true in another era.

The Backlash Against Women

Historically, women have avoided conflict in their roles as caretakers and guardians of relationships. One way they have been taught to do this is by backing down, or by taking a passive, one-down position. In what Susan Faludi has termed the recent backlash against the Feminist movement, some advice-givers, including former radio talk-show psychologist Dr. Toni Grant, have advocated adopting a passive stance to handle conflict. Basically, the suggestion is that women regress to the 1950s mentality of the traditional woman deferring to the big strong man.

Far from promising a winning plan for the 1990s, this strategy recalls the Victorian model and its kindred notion that one should be seen and not heard. What these authors fail to foresee is that if women adopt a passive strategy, they will make the problem worse. The more passive a woman becomes, the more dominant her spouse will become. Despite the appeal this may hold for men who are very insecure about their own authority and who feel that they need to dominate to be secure, this is not a successful coping strategy for most career women.

Blaming Women

Whenever anything goes wrong, most women blame themselves. If only they had been better mothers, better lovers, better listeners, then X, Y or Z wouldn't have happened. Or they think to themselves that if they hadn't been codependent, or so masochistic, they wouldn't have tolerated abusive relationships. Women tend to blame themselves for being single, or infertile, or for their marriages failing, or for their children being "at risk."

Society often encourages women to believe that they bring their problems upon themselves. The message girls receive is that they, not men, are responsible for making relationships work. The statement seems clear: "If you had been a good woman" (translated as a properly deferential person who took care of other people's needs ahead of your own), all this wouldn't have happened."

Even worse, many damaging myths are widely believed, such as "women really want to be raped," "women are abused because they are provocative," and "women are inherently masochistic."

While many women are indeed masochistic or co-dependent, they are not inherently so; they have been socialized to be that way. For example, one in three women was molested as a child. Women may indeed have a higher threshold for pain, because they were designed to endure childbirth, but this does not mean that they enjoy pain, or that they have a psychological wish to suffer.

Men Need Relationships Too

The traditional role separation holds lasting problems for both sexes. Some men have become so isolated from their families and themselves that they don't really know what it is they feel. When men who have spent so much energy being competitive and non-loving summarize their lives, they often ask themselves what was it all for? Was the price they paid for their success worth the estrangement from their families?

In a 1982 study on satisfaction, Bryant and Veroff found that marital dissatisfaction is one of the biggest factors leading to men's and women's overall feelings of discontent. Men do value their affiliations. Far from being the "independent" creatures portrayed in the old John Wayne movies, men are finding that without affiliations with women, other men, their children, or their families, their lives lack richness. As Sherman McCoy, the central character in Tom Wolfe's novel *Bonfire of Vanities*, discovered, life at the top without any relationships isn't worth much.

The research on how well men fare as singles is clear. Single men have a higher rate of alcoholism, drug abuse, and depression. Single, unattached, depressed males in their late forties and fifties are the highest risks for suicide. Undoubtedly, the rigid sex roles of the 1950s have shortchanged men as well as women. Having fewer friendships and feeling more reluctant to call on others for help, many men find themselves without the psychologically supporting friendships and resources most women employ. Far from being independent, men need women. It is this need for women, combined with their fears of engulfment, which creates the desire to dominate women.

Most men do not find it an agreeable state to be needy. The most common way for a man to handle feeling needy is to pair up with a woman who is even needier, so he can project his unwanted dependency onto her. She is the needy one; not he. The split continues; he is powerful and she is weak. He thinks, she feels. It isn't useful to continue to create stereotypes of gender along these lines. Both men and women think and feel, although women tend to describe their feelings better.

The time has come to stop perpetuating stereotypes of half-people. The first step out of the old sex role patterns is through self-awareness, which never comes from seeing yourself as incomplete.

Trying To Do It All

Women have traditionally been taught that their role in relationships is that of the caretaker, the nurturer. Men as well as women hold this expectation. This can become a problem for the career woman who believes that she must be the nurturer on top of all her other responsibilities. She then not only has to take charge in the office, but upon returning home, has to take charge of the relationship with the children, the husband, and the household. The so-called liberated woman in the workplace goes home to the not-so liberated position of caretaker, deferring her personal needs to the needs of others.

The psychological literature is full of studies of women who have attempted to meet all the expectations put upon them both internally (within their own value system) and externally (those placed on them by others and by society). The subject, "Roles, women and conflict," yielded 20,000 references in a computerized retrieval system of psychological articles and abstracts! The stress that accrues from this role struggle is also considerable. Most women attempting to fill all these roles wind up exhausted.

Carol, a physician, claimed, "I'm not a liberated woman. No woman who works and has children is liberated." There is no doubt that juggling multiple roles has its costs. The question is, do the benefits outweigh the costs? This question has been studied extensively by psychologists. The conclusions of Grace K. Barnett and Rosalind Baruch in articles which appeared in psychological journals in 1985, 1986, and 1987 were that the rewards outweigh the costs under the conditions in the following table.

Formula for Working Woman's Success

1. The husband is supportive of the wife working
2. Adequate childcare is available
3. Women work out of some element of choice as opposed to economic necessity

There are some who say that the conflicts of competing roles are too stressful for women. Yet others say that enhanced self esteem from increased status and privileges are a trade-off for the negative effects of juggling multiple roles. Of all the factors, being able to choose whether or not she works might be the most significant feature determining whether or not a woman is satisfied.

Women who work report that their sense of accomplishment is rewarding, while the most distressing aspects are role overload, role conflict, and the lack of career growth opportunities.

Some women choose to stay home and be mothers and home-makers even if they have the option of working. For the shrinking number of women who can afford this option, there are certain rewards and benefits. Yet, the majority of women (more than 60 percent of mothers work), do not have this choice. Spurred by a sagging economic climate, many families need two incomes to maintain the lifestyle they want for their families.

No More "Ozzie and Harriet"

Colorado Congresswoman Patricia Schroeder said, in an address to the American Association of Marriage and Family Therapists in 1989, that "America hasn't given up its image of 'Ozzie and Harriet,' but it isn't the norm any more."

Schroeder also said, "You can't go home again. You can't afford the American dream on one salary alone—the home, the car, the health insurance, college for the kids—but no one wants to redefine the dream."

The imperative for women to work to help support their families, is generally overlooked by the people who suggest that we return to the 1950s. The economics of the 1990s make this an impossible reality for most families. Accepting the fact that most women and mothers will work is a necessary societal adaptation. So, what are the conflicts which women who work face in relationships and how can these be worked out?

Approaches to Conflict

Leon Festinger, a social psychologist, wrote in 1957 that people deal with conflict in predictable ways. His theory was called "cognitive dissonance" and others since that time have broadened this into a theory of how people justify the discrepancies between their values and their behaviors.

The theory holds that when there are two competing ideas or behaviors, you will favor one and distance yourself from the other. In other words, people tend to avoid situations that cause them conflicts, or to change the meaning of the situations, or to manage to find these situations less aversive. Sometimes people even come to like and accept behavior or ideas which they once found repugnant.

Since women wish to avoid conflict, today's career women often use one of three basic strategies to avoid both conflict and feeling bad about themselves:

Strategy 1: Change Your Situation

Women have various options for changing their situation. The most common feature of this strategy is to remain single. The rationale women offer themselves to explain why they are single may vary, but this strategy explains why nearly 40 percent of today's executive women are single and why some divorcees don't care to remarry.

Another way in which women change their situation is to leave high status career jobs when they marry and have children. One reason they do this is to avoid the conflicts inherent in being a career woman, mother, and wife simultaneously.

Strategy 2: Change Your Behavior

Many authors advise women to change their behavior within their relationships. Toni Grant, in her best-selling book, *Being A Woman*, suggests reverting back to being the 1950s woman, by enhancing the dependent side of your personality. The rationale is that men prefer weaker women. The opposite strategy is more effective. Rather than becoming more passive, women should utilize problem-solving skills to work out the conflicts they face.

Strategy 3: Change Your Expectations

This is actually the simplest strategy, and yet it is the most profound. Accept conflict as part of your relationship, and learn ways to handle it and reduce its negative impact. No two individuals can remain separate individuals and avoid conflicts. We aren't alike enough, nor intuitive enough, nor perfectly willing to be selfless, nor giving enough to avoid conflict. But conflict doesn't have to mean battering. It doesn't mean there has to be a winner and a loser; it can also be just a difference of opinion.

Divorce

Since the 1960s, most women and men have adopted the attitude that it is easier to change relationships entirely than to live in conflictual relationships. This attitude took hold during an era of freedom when people believed they could enjoy free love (we have since learned that casual sex can have deadly consequences). The risks of divorce on children were downplayed. Marriage and family counselors were taught to advise couples to consider separation, rather than live in conflictual relationships. Two decades later, we see that children of divorce are scarred in ways no one anticipated and that second marriages end more often in divorce than first marriages. Seventy-six percent of step-families end in divorce court in less than seven years.

From the divorce literature, it is clear that although many divorced women describe themselves as happier, many have taken a plunge in their standard of living. Furthermore, while they have escaped the conflict with their husbands on an interactive level, the role overload of single motherhood is stressful as well.

The role conflicts of working women, particularly for working women with children, are both internal and external. Guilt over leaving their children each day and complex negotiations over whose job is it to do the housework and whose job is it to take care of the children need to be dealt with. The overload many working wives feel leads some to say the situation just isn't fair and so they leave their marriages, only to take their role overload with them.

The fantasy of most people seeking divorce is that life will be better; few anticipate it becoming worse. Some women divorce as a way to get away from a conflict regarding role overload. Husbands may have expected them to remain the same, while they wanted to change by altering their roles within the marriage and the world. In this situation, many women experience internal conflicts between what they expected themselves to be as wives and mothers, what they now want to be, and the pressure they feel when they go against their own training.

Although Shere Hite was discredited on the basis of biased sampling when her book, *Women in Love: A Cultural Revolution in Process*, came out in 1987, the central message her book addressed was women's dissatisfaction within romantic relationships. It is a fact that the divorce rate increased from 26 percent of all marriages in 1960 to nearly 50 percent for most of the 1980s. Although not all divorces are initiated by women, these numbers suggest that there is some correlation with women's dissatisfaction and their increased means to leave if they are dissatisfied.

The more women achieve in their careers, the higher their chances are for divorce. A survey of highly educated women earning more than $20,000 a year reveals a divorce rate four times higher than for those who earn less, according to Andrew Cherlin.

For some divorced women, the major task is to heal their own wounds, and to learn the skills necessary to avoid repeating the same mistakes. Some women in this category protect themselves by being too critical; no man is good enough. Others recognize that they just aren't ready to reexperience any of their previous pain; staying single is a safe alternative.

Single Career Women

One of the most common explanations for why so many successful career women are single is that men are threatened by them. The assumption is that these women want men but that the men won't have them. But the reverse is often true. There are men who would be happy to be with these women; the women don't wish to be with these men. The women may feel on some level that "No one is good enough," or that they would have to compromise too much.

What do they mean by compromise? Most, in order to find a man, would have to abandon the 1950s standard of older, taller, richer, and smarter, and they are unwilling to do that. Others feel overwhelmed by the conflict between being a career woman at work, and a relational woman at home. They think that in order to do both, they have to give up a part of themselves.

Diane, a single parent in her thirties, was a very successful businesswoman, and very masculine in her attributes. She had one relationship after another. After two years with any one man, she got bored. The men never seemed to be as strong or as aggressive as she was. Although Diane had developed her masculine side, the part that was aggressive, courageous, and initiatory, she was constantly disappointed because the men she met could never outdo her. When she met one who could, she branded him a male chauvinist pig or criticized him for his poor relationship skills. She was constantly frustrated in her efforts to find a man more masculine than she was.

Through her work in therapy, it became clear that her desire to find someone to dominate her was part of how she had learned to get in touch with her feeling side. When she was the one on top, she had trouble experiencing herself as a feeling and nurturing person. She had learned to be in touch with her own feminine side only through a complementary interaction with a man. He led, and she followed. After she learned some techniques to shift into her feminine side, she found that she could then be with a different type of man. When she was finally able to let go of her past expectations, she began a relationship with a man whose feelings and intuition were dominant personality traits. Eventually they married.

This view of roles within a relationship is characteristic of women raised in the 1950s.   Being female is the opposite of being male. The way masculine and feminine traits are described takes on a polarity in which the masculine set of attributes or behaviors evokes and complements the feminine set of attributes or behaviors.   Women too frequently rely on being the opposite of a man to experience their own femininity.

Some single career women don't know how to have a relationship with a man without giving up the person they experience themselves to be.   In other words, the internal model they hold about what the role of a woman is supposed to be differs so markedly from how they experience themselves that the solution they adopt is to avoid relationships, because the relationships cause them conflict.   It may be that they experience conflict between themselves and the man, but frequently the conflict is internal as well; it is their own experience of themselves in the relationship which they wish to avoid.

Paula, 38, an accountant, was brought up in a traditional family in which her mother was deferential and passive and her father was dominant.   As the oldest of three, Paula also filled the role of caretaker in the family.

In her adult life, Paula has vowed consciously to not become a woman like her mother, nor to end up as a man's caretaker. Unfortunately, the major model she observed about how to be a woman in a relationship involved being deferential and being the caretaker.   Paula gets involved with men, but she usually leaves the relationship when she finds the man becoming too dominant and herself becoming too passive.   She doesn't like how this feels, and since she doesn't know how to do it differently, she feels better about herself when she is alone.   At least she sees herself as strong, assertive, independent, and smart.   She is a terrific friend, but she does admit that it gets lonely.   She fears that if she brings a man into her life, that she'll compromise herself too much.

This is a protective stance for Paula.   When the relationship gets too close, she gets insecure that she will become a woman like her mother and lose herself in the process. The way in which she protects herself is not to let men get too close.

The Not-So-Liberated Woman

You may recall that Matina Horner suggested that women eschewed success because they perceived success as conflicting with their role as females.   Success was viewed as hierarchical; if you got to the top it meant that someone else was displaced in the process. The idea of succeeding at someone else's expense was viewed as conflict-producing, because good women took care of others first. This was the ethic of care described by Carol Gilligan in her popular 1982 book, In *A Different Voice*.

Horner theorized that a perceived conflict between self and other was the source of the fear of success in women. For some women, the solution was to avoid careers and anything they construed as making themselves stand out. They may have avoided conflict, but they avoided much of the richness of life as well.

Paula chose the opposite approach. She wanted to pursue a career, and she likes what the career has done for her identity and her self-esteem. In fact, she identified with the career role more than she identifies with the role of wife or mother. She'd like to have children, but she doesn't know how to make the transition from being a career woman into being a married woman without losing a part of herself. She has mastered her fear of success in terms of her career, but her fear of losing herself in a relationship still looms large.

In 1982, psychiatrist Juri Willi found that women behaved more deferentially when they were with their husbands than when they were alone. By giving women and men joint Rorschach tests ("ink blot" tests used to identify personality characteristics), he found that women lowered their level of functioning when they were with their husbands, while men scored the same whether or not their wives were present.

This is exactly what Paula is afraid of, that she will lose some part of herself in a relationship. Paula, who prides herself on her status and her identity as a professional, fears becoming suddenly less than who she is in order to be in a relationship. This is too high a price to pay. Hence, the conflict between how she views herself as a career woman and how she would perceive herself in a relationship is so disturbing that she avoids the whole issue in order to protect herself. Unfortunately, she ends up feeling lonely.

Looking For Perfection

Another way to avoid internal and external conflict is to look for too much in one person. Career women frequently criticize men for not being enough. The criticism might be "he isn't strong enough, rich enough, sexy enough, emotional enough." A protection some women employ is to make the standards so high or so unrealistic that no man is ever able to meet them. It's a version of the "yes, but" game. "He's nice, but he's not _____." Whether they are protecting themselves from an internal conflict like Paula, who doesn't know how to be what she wants to be in a relationship, or protecting themselves from being hurt again, like the divorcee who's not recovered from the pain of breakup and loss, or whether the conflict is more external, they see the men who they attract as less than they are. No one is ever good enough.

Barbara, a 30-year-old single broadcast executive, says, "I want a man who is macho enough that he feels he is smarter, stronger, and in control, yet sensitive enough that he will relate to my feelings and be able to talk about his feelings...but not so sensitive that he is a wimp...." Setting her goal so high will make it hard for Barbara to find a living, breathing human being—available or not—who meets her specific, and often contradictory, criteria.

Does Money Matter?

Leslie, 39, is a successful businesswoman. She's pretty and she's strong. She says that her main problem is finding men who earn more money than she does. She thinks she is supposed to marry up (marry a man who is richer). But she makes so much money herself, that to find a man who makes more is very difficult. She has narrowed the pool to about one or two percent of the available men.

To complicate things further, she'd really like the man to be older, but not so old that he won't agree to have children. And she would also like him to be taller and certainly smarter. Now, she might be able to handle slightly younger, or shorter, but smarter and richer are two important criteria for her. Why?

If she doesn't marry a man who has more resources than she does, she will have to deal with the conflict of her old values against her new reality. One of the things has to go: either the values will have to be revised, or she will have to change her behavior and only date men who are like the men her mother would have chosen for her. She's in a values clash. Internally, she knows that some of these guys aren't right for her. But she bought into an image—from television, movies and books—about what a family was supposed to look like. She expects to recreate the relationship modeled by her parents when she was growing up. She's used to having power, but she expects that the man she will eventually be with will have more. She hasn't really ever thought about marrying an equal. She's not sure how that would work.

Scenario: Female art director, 40, married to a man in the music business. She bought the house with her money before they married and asked him to sign a prenuptial agreement agreeing that he had no right to the house should they ever separate. Her higher earnings caused bad feelings for the duration of the relationship and eventually they divorced.

Men routinely, if sometimes resentfully, share their higher wages with their wives. Are women as willing to do so? Among the couples interviewed for this book, the wives who had no problem sharing their resources appeared to be happier in their marriages than those who were more reluctant or resentful about sharing something which they felt on some level to be inappropriate.

If you asked the art director in this scenario, she would say that all men are uncomfortable being with women who earn more money than they do. All men? It depends on which ones you ask. The men who don't feel threatened by a woman's greater earnings—and they exist—tend to have one thing in common; they feel secure about themselves as men.

"If she always has to have her own way or is constantly in my face about how she earns more, and is always talking about how I'm not enough, who needs this?" asked Warren, a 43-year-old man. "But if she treats me with respect and we share her money as well as mine, who cares who makes it?"

Money is frequently a vehicle for status and control in a marriage, with the higher wage earner commanding more status and control. At least, that was the power arrangement of the complementary marriages of the 1950s. The last place anyone wants to see themselves is at the bottom or lower rung. No one likes to be in the one-down position. But the men interviewed for this book never saw themselves as inferior, despite the fact that their wives earned more money than they did. Indeed, many clung to the traditional image of male superiority in the working world.

"This is just a transition," said Joe, a 39-year-old therapist. "She makes $100,000 in her sales job and I make only $85,000, but I've got more potential."

Also, Joe insisted, "While she makes more money and she's good at what she does, she sees my work as more important in the overall scheme of things. Our shared perception is that my work is more valuable to society."

Joe says one of the things he likes best about his wife is that "She is independent and quite capable of taking care of herself. Part of my choice in picking her was that it was important to me to be with a strong woman who could be a teammate and share in building a financial structure so we can accomplish things we want in life. Given the present economy, and the reality of making money in the 1990s, I think that is the realistic perspective to have. Both partners have to work if you want to get ahead and you want to accomplish things." Whether they saw themselves as equals or not, the financial reality was that she made more; and he felt just fine about it.

Central to the backlash against feminism is the theme that working women threaten men and the stability of marriages. But unlike the popular perception, many men you speak to say that the independence of their wives is an asset instead of a liability.

Mike, a composer, says, "I can't imagine being married to someone who wasn't my equal. I couldn't imagine even going out with a victim type... Even when I was younger, I always wanted to be with a woman who had a good sense of her self-worth."

Steve, married for the second time, said, "My nature is not to be confrontational, but if something really bothers me, I can stand my ground."

"I don't view romantic relationships between men and women as very different from platonic relationships, with sex added. I don't think there should be a different power structure than there would be between friends of the same sex. If we have differences, we battle them out," Mike said.

What Are Your Options?

As you can see, today's career woman faces considerable clashes in values and expectations.   The demands of the modern working world require very different skills and attitudes than the demands of the traditional romantic relationship, but these conflicts can be solved in a variety of ways.   The three primary approaches to conflict resolution are explored below.

Option 1: Change Your Situation— Keep the Relationship and Drop the Career

Alissa was a successful business woman when she married Bob. She felt very comfortable getting married, but after the birth of her first child she decided to quit work and devote herself to her children.   Having been brought up in a fairly traditional family, Alissa valued family life. She now has three children and is happy. She drives them to their sports games and other after-school activities, and plans her life around her kids and her social life. The only problem is that Alissa is always gaining weight and then trying to lose it.   Asked why she gave up her career, she said they didn't need the money, and if she worked, who would be there to raise the children? When pressed further, she suggested that she would be very uncomfortable with having a job which competed with the needs of her family and her husband. What she didn't say was that her previous job carried more status than her husband's current job. She didn't even acknowledge that this was an issue.

Two psychologists, Dana Vannoy-Hiller and William W. Philliber, in their book *Equal Partners*, suggested that one way in which career women handled the conflict in having more status or financial earning power than their husbands was simple; they just left their careers and took jobs which didn't challenge their husband's status or self esteem.

For many women, family life is the career of choice.   If they work, they feel very conflicted.   In such cases, devoting oneself exclusively to raising a family is a fine choice.   But women who derive identity and self-worth through work had best think twice about this option.

Option 2: Change Your Behavior

The message of some psychologists is to return to the values of the 1950s. In her book, *Being A Woman*, Toni Grant advises women to act like courtesans, because men are threatened by independent women. She cautions women about going too far and becoming "Amazons," women who have little use for men. The very sad and confusing thing is that part of her message is true; there are some women who have gone too far, and some men are threatened by independent women. (Actually the phrase, "independent women", is a misnomer, for it implies that women choose to be without men. A more constructive phrase might be "interdependent women", women who are capable of functioning on their own, but also choose to be in relationships for their nurturing and family needs.)

It's not that the courtesan isn't appealing to men; men have always appreciated women who were willing to buoy their egos by making a man the center of their world. But to suggest to all women that this is the solution is ludicrous.

The 1950s solution, with its clearly delineated roles, evolved into lopsided relationships between men and women in terms of power and control, denial and repression. This was followed by the wild relational experimentation of the 1960s. The rigidity of traditional sex roles had proved explosively unfulfilling, and certainly the high divorce rate which followed the 1950s indicated something about how desirable an arrangement almost 50 percent of married people felt they had.

It is always easier to follow the known pathways, the stereotypes of "proper" role behavior, than it is to find your own way. But even if you want to, you can't turn the clock back. Once their eyes have been opened to what it means to have their own identities, would women, if they could, turn back?

Toni Grant's assumption is that women don't want to have their own identities; they will be happy being the mirror image of their husbands' needs. She suggests that career women are possessed by a negative animus. Translated into simpler language, this means that their masculine side, rather than being integrated into their personalities, is outside of their awareness. This exposed masculine side serves to drive their personalities in a critical and demanding way.

This is an oversimplification and a misuse of Jung's concept of the animus. Toni Grant limits a woman's masculine side (her animus) to the "Amazon". This wasn't Jung's idea of the animus, which he saw as the unconscious part of her feminine identification. It is through the masculine that women experience their authority and their competence. The Amazon, when integrated, helps expand feminine identification. One isn't either an Amazon or a courtesan; one passes through all these as phases, the courtesan, the Amazon, the wise old woman, and the mother. Jung never intended it to be conceptualized as an either/or choice. Becoming whole isn't about splitting off parts of yourself. It is about encompassing, including, and integrating different parts of yourself. It is the ability to encompass, include, and integrate that makes women uniquely feminine. To treat the animus as though it were an alien intruder only serves to push it further into the unconscious, where it exerts more, not less, control over your life. If women were to give up the Amazon aspect of their masculine identities, they would lose the capacity to function as autonomous people.

The idea isn't to be stuck in any one stage of identification. Being stuck in the Amazon stage can be as stultifying as being stuck in the mother stage. The positive function of the Amazon is to bring women into their own identities and help them find their own voices. There is, of course, a negative side to any trait. But the goal shouldn't be to exclude your masculine side; rather it should be to incorporate and include it into your self-concept so you can be masculine and independent when you choose to be, and feminine and receptive when you choose to be.

One way in which some career women protect themselves from leaving the realm of this Amazon masculine identification is to be overly critical of men. It is a trait of the negative animus to be particularly critical and demeaning. Unfortunately, these opinions are registered as facts; there appears to be no outside awareness that these are just mere opinions. "He's not good enough," "Men aren't strong enough," "They don't make enough money," "All they want is to have control."

When a woman is being this critical, more often than not she is protecting herself from internal dissatisfaction. Rather than seeing it internally, she criticizes whomever is on the outside (husbands, children, friends, relatives). This is unpleasant and ultimately counterproductive, since few people respond well to being criticized. Frequently women are overly critical because of a conflict between their masculine side—which seeks separation—and their feminine side—which seeks connectedness. Being overly critical doesn't resolve these opposing forces.

Option 3: Change Your Expectations

Most couples initially share the fantasy that a good relationship doesn't involve conflict. In the past much of the domain of relationships was taken for granted; women were the caretakers and were deferential towards their husbands, who had the last word. Despite many unconscious and even conscious desires to form and reform relationships based on this old pattern, there are many men and women who, having seen the flaws in the system, want to have their relationships work differently.

One of the issues that couples and singles need to address is the difference between what they want to have and what they were taught they wanted to have. They need to separate what might work for them now, from what they expect should work. The common belief that women believe should marry someone older, taller, richer, and smarter is a knee-jerk response. It is only through close examination, perhaps initiated through a failure to obtain what they wanted from a man they thought was Mr. Right, that women are able to change what they want and in turn expect from Mr. Right.

Beth, the surgeon who married her mother's ideal son-in-law and then found that he didn't meet her own needs, chose for her second husband a man who understood the demands of her career.

Gloria, an attorney whose first husband was also an attorney who expected her to rush home from court to put dinner on the table, chose for her second husband a man who earned less money than she did, but who shared the household chores with her and filled her emotional and familial needs better.

Arlene, a college professor, realized that if she had an IQ of 150, that meant that only about one percent of the male population was smarter than she was. Since she earned nearly $100,000 a year, she figured that if she looked for a man who earned more, that narrowed the pool even more. Finally she decided that it was unrealistic to expect that a man who was older, smarter, and richer was also going to be able to meet her emotional needs. She chose instead a man with several academic degrees who earned less than she did and was a few years younger.

"I realized I didn't have to have a man who was smarter than I am, just one who was smart enough. And he didn't have to earn more money, he just had to earn enough. And he didn't have to have a better job, he just had to have a good enough job," she said.

The Internal Battle of the 1950s Wife & the 1990s Woman

There are many ways in which the conflict between being the girl your 1950s mother taught you to be conflicts with being the 1990s career woman. It can be handled by turning it inward, and avoiding relationships. It can be acted out through adopting negative and demeaning attitudes towards men. It can be acted out through external battles for control and respect with your partner.

The only way to win the battle is first to conquer the conflict internally. Once you have your own negative animus under control, *meaning you aren't criticizing yourself for not being a better woman,* you can begin to work out problems between you and your mate. Many problems arise because the woman isn't hearing criticism only on the outside, but she is also criticizing herself on the inside. This combination is a sure killer of any self-esteem or any ability to handle the situation in a winning fashion.

CHAPTER SIX

Sexual Issues:
The Myth of Fleeing Men
& Suffocating Women

"I think men are basically sexual animals, and I feel like part of me is too," said Jill, a 34-year-old bookkeeper. "I still have a hard time reconciling my own needs. I have a hard time being affectionate with a man, without being a tease. I have trouble drawing the line, saying, 'I'll go this far, but I don't want to sleep with you.'"

Many women share the pain and anguish Jill describes in trying to reconcile her sexual needs, her conflicting mores, her desire for a relationship, and her recently acquired fear of sexually transmitted diseases. Coming to adolescence in the early 1970s, Jill believed that, if she were attracted to a man, it was okay to sleep with him, maybe even on a first date. She felt she had a right to engage in casual sex just the way men did, and she didn't worry about the consequences. After all, she was on the pill.

Things were different in her mother's day. Then the rules were very simple. There were good girls and bad girls, and the good girls waited. The fiction was that only sluts had sex outside of marriage. The reality was that most women withheld sex at least until they felt they were in a committed relationship. The pressure to remain chaste came partly from the culture, and partly from fear of consequences that far outweighed any other concerns. Lack of reliable contraception made unwanted pregnancy a very real risk in premarital sex. The fact that abortion was against the law in the United States gave women few options. Engaging in sex could force a woman into a situation in which she either endangered her life by an illegal abortion, or had to go into hiding before bearing an illegitimate child and then giving it up for adoption, or entered into a "shotgun wedding."

An unwanted pregnancy could stigmatize her forever in her community, prevent her from finishing her education, or lead her into a premature and possibly unhappy marriage. Divorce was as scandalous as illegitimacy, and as a result many couples who got married only because there was a child on the way stayed together for the rest of their lives. No wonder the smart thing for a woman to do was to withhold sex until she was sure she loved the guy and that he would stand by her. The only reliable contraceptive a woman could control by herself was a diaphragm, which required a doctor's visit and prior planning. Even the use of a condom required a break in the action that gave her some time to consider her actions. In order to explain why a woman would be so foolish as to give in to her own sexual desire, considering the potential consequences, she needed to be able to rationalize it to herself and to others, by being "swept away" by passion and romantic feelings. But the fear of pregnancy was strong enough that most women needed no other excuse for chastity.

"I remember being with Bill in the back seat of a parked car on a country road in 1958," recalls Cathy, now in her fifties. "I really loved him, and I wanted to have sex with him. What stopped me was the fear that if we had sex even once, I would wind up pregnant, we'd both have to quit school, and he'd spend the rest of his life working as a gas station attendant to support us. I knew he loved me and would not abandon me to face the consequences alone, but the absolute certainty that giving in to our desires was going to destroy both our lives certainly extinguished my ardor."

Changing Rules

During the social upheaval of the 1960s and 1970s, a lot of rules changed in contemporary society. The Civil Rights Movement, the Women's Liberation Movement, and the Anti-Vietnam War protests led to liberalized attitudes. Concurrently, the birth control pill became widely available, allowing women like Cathy to take precautions that separated the issues of pregnancy from those of having sex.

As abortion became legal and available throughout most of the United States in the late 1960s and early 1970s, the threat of unplanned pregnancy became less terrifying. For the first time, women had sexual options, and they began to exercise them. Not until the fatal consequences of unprotected sex began to be widely publicized with the advent of AIDS in the 1980s did the sexual revolution begin to slow down.

It was during the sexual liberation movement of the 1960s and 1970s that women and men experimented with altering the sexual agreement of the 1950s. Freed from the fear of pregnancy by enhanced contraception, women for the first time entered colleges in the same proportion as men and began to think of themselves as equal to men in their access to education, careers, and perhaps even sex. Women began behaving in similar ways to men. They sometimes initiated sex, and they wanted to be sure that they too had orgasms. There was more candid sex education for women and more acceptance of women enjoying their sexuality. A book called *Our Bodies, Ourselves*, published by the Boston Women's Health Book Collective, taught women how to examine their own genitalia, and popular books such as *For Yourself Only*, by Lonnie Barbach, *The Hite Report on Female Sexuality*, by Shere Hite, and *Men and Sexuality*, by Bernie Ziebergeld, encouraged a new openness about sexuality.

For some women, acting more like men worked out fine. They balanced their careers and their commitment to the man (or men) in their lives without too much *Sturm und Drang*. Another group of women, however, came out of the 1960s and 1970s feeling betrayed and confused. Now in their thirties and forties, with their biological clocks chiming in the background, they felt that the 1960s rhetoric about equality was hogwash. Men their age weren't feeling the same crunch about child-bearing. These were the women who panicked with the hysteria that greeted the Harvard-Yale study, which purported to prove that women of their age had lost their chance to grab the matrimonial brass ring. Many of them believed the dire predictions, although there have been arguments that the predictions had more to do with a feminist backlash that blamed women for valuing their careers too much than with predicting their marital success rates.

Most of the women who felt betrayed by the sexual revolution have had a series of relationships. Some have been married, many have dated or been involved in live-in arrangements of varying lengths. They are sexually sophisticated, but ambivalent about what they want from a relationship. Most want a committed relationship, but not the oppressive variety. For many women, sex for sex's sake is shallow. They seek a more profound bond, and are dubious of sexual intimacy producing emotional intimacy and commitment. They have shared sex with a man with the implicit understanding that a relationship would follow, but what happened instead was an approach-avoidance dance characterized by women complaining that men were unable to commit and that they had been betrayed.

"Swept Away"

In her 1984 book, *Swept Away*, Carol Cassell discusses the strong need women have to be in love or in a relationship before they have sex. One way they have been trained to deal with the conflict between their erotic desires and their need for relationships in which to contain their vulnerability is through denial. They cloak their drives in romance. Instead of admitting that they participated in a sexual relationship because they wanted to have sex with the man, they rationalized that they did it because they were swept away by the passion of the moment, which, of course, was the result of deep feelings they both shared. They created wishful but fictitious relationships out of one-night stands, and rationalized their sexual encounters by fantasizing that they were simply overwhelmed by their feelings of love.

Cassell says the feeling of being swept away is a disguise for a woman's true erotic feelings, which she has been socialized to describe as romance. For the brief moments of sexual euphoria, women trade long hours of depression, anger, and hostility when an encounter doesn't follow the fictitious course they've plotted.

Other authors have also developed Cassell's theme. In *Human Sexuality*, James McCary found that a woman must be "carried away" to avoid "planned sex." In *Veiled Contract*, Greer Litton Fox wrote that for an unmarried woman to engage in premarital sex, she must feel she is swept away by the passion of the moment. Fox says that sex is a gift a woman bestows on a man, which in turn puts him in her debt. He is supposed to repay her with love, devotion, and future commitment.

In the past, these rules were clear. The sexual revolution changed the rules for many men and women, but for some women, this contractual agreement still operates on a subconscious level. They blame men for not living up to an agreement the men didn't know they were making. In fact, in some cases not only had the men not agreed to it, but they had overtly stated their objections.

Women had approached the relationship assuming that there would be an equal distribution of power and control, only to discover that their own need to be contained pushed the man to insist on defending his own need for autonomy. Rather than getting the relationship they were looking for, the women felt abused and misused.

Few women, however, recognized that they had contributed to the misunderstanding. When women went outside of this 1950s bargaining stance, they also gave away most of their bargaining power. The betrayal women felt when they realized that they had traded sex for a relationship that existed only in their own fantasies is as much an internal as an external betrayal. No longer protected by the sexual bargaining which had been the mainstay of the ethics of the 1950s, in which women withheld sex until they felt secure in a relationship, women had relied on what they thought was good will.

Psychological & Gender Issues Surrounding Sex

While men and women may not be so different in their desire to be loved and valued, they are tremendously different in the meaning they attach to their sexuality. Men aren't necessarily inclined to make sexual relationships into love relationships, although some men do this in the same way women do. Certainly the masculine stereotype is that men are independent and only reluctantly wooed into relationships. Consequently, men have retained an ability to view sex as sex and not necessarily as a step into a relationship. As Cassell points out, "Unless a relationship is well established, it is more than likely that sex for a man will be unconnected with being in, feeling, or looking for love." Along with this notion of masculinity, men learn that control and autonomy are the essence of manhood. Whereas women characterize sex and sharing as being vulnerable, men are taught to fear this state.

Clearly some of the psychological issues surrounding sex are different for men and women and are even oppositional. Sexuality represents many things, as the chart reveals.

As you can see, many of the reasons people engage in sex have little to do with creating intimacy. But what women repeatedly report is their desire to experience intimacy with sex. This may not

Reasons People Have Sex
Excitement
Danger (Infidelity)
Love
Sharing
Caring
Touching
The Need to Feel Needed
Validation of Sexual Attractiveness
Conquest
Release of Tension
Escape from Depression
Expression of Independence (Infidelity)
Avoidance of Emotional Intimacy
Lust
Infatuation
Boredom
Recreation
Variety
Retaliation for Spouse's Affair (Infidelity)
Provision of Sex not Available in Another Relationship (Infidelity)

be what most men want out of a casual sexual encounter. The sex act, very intimate by nature, becomes the arena in which both men and women act out their psychological issues. Because men and women are so different in their archetypal issues around what it means to connect to another person, a foray into understanding their different psychological make-ups is in order.

Men and Autonomy

Most men grow up with their mother as their primary nurturing figure, the person in the world to whom they are most attached. But at around four or five years old, they realize that they are not the same as Mother. They construct an identity that pushes Mother away. In order to establish their sexual identity, they must also establish autonomy.

The archetypical issues of the separation from Mother are illustrated in the male mythology of the hero Achilles, who goes off to fight the war in *The Iliad*. Robert Johnson, in his book, *He*, defines the various acts of heroism in battle as archetypal ways in which men create a separate identity. Men struggle and hopefully resolve the issue of being separate. When these issues remain unresolved, being too close to a woman may bring up feelings of engulfment. Most men choose to flee to regain their own boundaries. Whenever closeness is experienced as engulfment, the negative side of the mother complex is present (whether it is experienced by a man or a woman).

The negative mother complex threatens one's right to exist. It is a feeling of being annihilated. The man or woman in the grips of a negative mother complex sees himself or herself as too small for the task. Unable to satisfy the devouring Mother, the man (or woman) feels shame, and ultimately flees the relationship which feels stifling, too close, or, as some men have described it, like "a black hole."

Although this is mainly true for men, it can happen to women too, as it did to Elaine, a 37-year-old nightclub singer. Elaine internalized the change in sex roles to the extreme degree that, in her sexual relationships with men, she behaved more like a man than a woman. She enjoyed the company of men, and she enjoyed sex, but she avoided committed relationships. When a man got too close to Elaine, she felt smothered. She found most relationships with men too constraining.

Elaine is the exception, and not all men experience intimacy this way either, but men who are insufficiently confident of their abilities to negotiate this psychological motif, or who are unable to maintain sufficient boundaries, are the ones women refer to as "commitment phobic." They fear becoming too close to a woman; they fear the loss of their autonomy, which is the symbol of their masculine self.

This need for autonomy can get acted out in ways which surprise the woman, who may not in any way intend to control the man. If a woman makes what she thinks to be an innocuous request, such as, "Call and let me know what time you are going to be home," the man may hear it as a threat to his independence, particularly if he interprets it as limiting his control. He may also feel that checking with his wife or girlfriend before inviting friends over to the house is a threat to his autonomy. He may feel that he needs the freedom to make the decision himself. Usually, if the mother complex is fairly resolved, and if the woman explains that she is not trying to control him, the man can snap out of it. But some men can't.

An extreme example was Nick, 39, who was feeling lost in his new marriage. He came home one night and casually mentioned to his wife that he had decided to go to New York for three months to live. He didn't understand why she got upset. He wasn't ending the relationship; he just wanted to spend some time on a project in New York, and needed to feel that he had control over his own life and his decisions.

Unfortunately, she didn't see it the same way. She experienced his decision as an abandonment of the relationship. Both were able to see their competing needs. She needed to have this be a joint decision. He was adamant that he needed to go. She agreed, but insisted that he must keep in touch by calling her two or three times a week. He agreed, but when he got to New York, he failed to keep his promise. This left her feeling abandoned again, and she filed for divorce before he got home.

Women and Containment

Containment is a major issue for women. The sexual act involves a literal intrusion into their bodies, which most women experience, consciously or unconsciously, as making them vulnerable. Most feel a need for a relationship to surround, contain, and protect this vulnerable state. In order to feel comfortable in a sexual relationship, they have a deep-seated need to feel protected and valued. Women constantly say that for them to feel like having sex, they need to feel emotionally connected.

Like men, women are almost always raised by their mothers, but unlike men, it is all right for them to identify with their mothers. Separation is not the main issue for little girls or for women. Instead, the major theme for women is maintaining connections. In her book, *In a Different Voice*, Carol Gilligan wrote that the feminine personality defines itself in relation and connection to other people more than the masculine personality does.

"Consequently," she wrote, "relationships, and particularly issues of dependency, are experienced differently by women and men. For boys and men, separation and individuation are critically tied to gender identity since separation from the mother is essential for the development of masculinity. For girls and women, issues of femininity or feminine identity do not depend on the achievement of separation from the mother or on the progress of individuation.... Since masculinity is defined through separation while femininity is defined through attachment, male gender identity is threatened by intimacy while female gender identity is threatened by separation. Thus males tend to have difficulty with relationships, while females tend to have problems with individuation."

In the late 1960s, as mentioned earlier, psychologist Erik H. Erikson suggested that men find out who they are before they are really able to enter into an intimate relationship with a woman. Women, on the other hand, put off developing a separate identity until they find a man to marry them and provide them with part of their identity. For men identity precedes intimacy according to this model. For men identity also precedes generativity (the passing of the torch to subsequent generations, both through procreation and through the teaching of accumulated wisdom). For women these tasks seem instead to be fused. Intimacy goes along with identity, as the female comes to know herself as she is known, through her relationships with others.

When Nick announced, as a way of showing his independence, that he was moving to New York for three months, his decisions triggered his wife's anxieties about abandonment. As he became increasingly remote in his decisions and in his willingness to share his feelings about his need for separateness, it became increasingly difficult for her to feel contained and safe in the relationship. His need to be autonomous directly conflicted with her need to be contained. This is an archetypal battle between the sexes.

Certainly, among young women who have not created an identity for themselves, and among young men not yet secure in their independence and autonomy, the male's resistance to commitment is at cross-purposes with a woman's psychological need for commitment to surround the vulnerability she experiences around sex.

Much of the wisdom about women's and men's feelings about sexuality and identity is based on men and women developing intimate relationships in their twenties. It does not necessarily fit the current reality of men and women who are single in their thirties and forties, who have fully formed separate identities and have resolved some of their issues during a earlier marriages or serious relationships. Singles in their forties are less likely to have the same fears they had in their twenties. A man who has been married before or who has had long relationships is unlikely to have as strong a fear of commitment as a younger man does, although for some die-hard bachelors, these fears are still prominent. Women who have remained single long enough to build a career are likely to have created an identity for themselves apart from their relationship to men. Many divorced women, who have survived a first marriage and its break-up, have achieved an identity apart from their former spouses.

For these post-identity couples, the issues are less about fear of commitment and more about what the new remarried family will look like and to whom they are making commitments. Him, his children, me, my children, his career, my career? For career men and women in their forties, relationships in the 1990s are very different from the relationship issues of people in their twenties who haven't yet resolved the issues of "Who am I?" and "What is my sexuality all about?"

Moving Towards the New Sexual Contract

The sexual contract of the 1950s was based on a style of relationship with rigidly defined roles and called for women to trade sex for security. Then came the free sex engendered by the so-called Sexual Revolution. This sexual contract of the 1960s and 1970s is unrealistic in the age of AIDS. What needs to come now is a new understanding of sexual roles. The new sexual contract needs to take into account the different needs and different psychological drives of men and women, with their similar struggles for power, recognition, and intimacy. The goal of the new contract is to be able to shift from having opposite needs to acknowledging their mutual struggle. While the old contract was based on pre-defined and rigid role expectations, each new contract must be individually negotiated between two people, and take into account their individual needs and their needs as a couple.

Men and women react differently to certain situations, particularly those framed in terms of control, independence or dependence, dominance or submission. But even though the sexes bring different archetypal issues to each experience and thus react differently, it is important to remember that men and women are also similar. What this means is that both have needs for intimacy and closeness. Both wish to have the feeling of kinship and companionship. Both want to share life's experiences.

The methods are different, but the goals are the same.

Resolving Conflict

Nick and his wife became polarized around his need for autonomy and her need for containment. Whenever two people are engaged in a complementary relationship, each person's needs tend to polarize the other into a more extreme version of the opposite quality.

The more Nick pushed for independence, the more his wife felt threatened and needed to know the boundaries of their relationship. The more she pushed for containment, the more evasive Nick became. The only way out of a circular transaction like this, in which each person's response magnifies and brings out the other's fears, is to step outside of the dynamic. There are at least three good ways to do this:

1. Reframe the Problem

When a couple gets polarized around any issue, a good way to deal with the problem is to change the definition of the problem into something more manageable. It isn't about his need for independence versus her need for containment; rather they are enacting archetypal issues around their masculinity and their femininity. (This in part removes each of them as the driver of the dynamic, but may not be enough to shift their stances.) Another way to reframe the problem is to speak of this as a battle for control. If both were more secure, they'd give the other more psychological room.

2. Move Toward Common Ground

Usually, the best way to break a circular and complementary interaction is to move towards the common ground. How are the two parties similar? Are both afraid of being too close? How does each person's fear of intimacy push them to react like this? When the relationship was working, what was different? In the past he was able to tell her about his plans. Why then and not now? How did she respond to him that made it seem safer? And for her, when was he able to exclude her from his plans without making her afraid? What made it okay then? In thinking about a past time when each was able to do exactly the same thing and yet get a different response, what made that situation different?

3. Use Different Language

Norm, 44, is an attorney who is afraid of marriage. He describes his fear as a "black hole." Every marriage he has seen involves two unhappy people. The wife nags the husband; the husband withdraws from the wife. They get locked into this circular pattern in which one's nagging evokes the other's withdrawal; it becomes a no-win situation.

Norm fears that since this is the only interaction he has seen, this is what will also happen to him. Because he is an attorney, the suggestion was made that he see marriage as a contract and that he use his negotiation skills to draw up his own contract. Because his language is one of contracts, negotiations, renegotiations and arbitrations, he can use this understanding to describe a different vision of what relationships can be. Redefining marriage as a process in which both partners create a mutually satisfactory relationship gives both parties some control. This was a prospect Norm found more appealing. Think about how the other person thinks and cast both your sides in those terms.

Different Rules, Same Game

Eleanor Maccoby studied how boys and girls play differently, and pointed out that boys are more likely to play highly structured games in which the rules are very clearly defined. When there was a conflict during the play, boys usually dealt with it, so the game could go on. Girls, on the other hand, were more likely to play in smaller groups, in an unstructured fashion, without rules. When there was a conflict, girls tended to stop playing. The funny thing is that when young men and women grow up and interact with one another, the opposite phenomenon occurs.

In her book, *You Just Don't Understand*, Deborah Tannen points out that men and women approach conversations with very different rules about dominance, hierarchy, and negotiation. Women frequently try to get the man to speak emotionally, be emotionally supportive, come forth with some feeling.

According to the research of John Gottman, who took physiological measurements of couples quarreling, men experience conflict as more physiologically arousing than women. They not only get more aroused, but it takes them longer to come back to a normal state. Gottman referred to the avoidance of this aroused state as "stonewalling." Men avoid conflict rather than getting themselves all riled up. Women, however, are left miffed by what they perceive as a male unwillingness to fully participate in a conflict with them.

Psychologist Howard Markman, developer of a structured course in conflict resolution called "PAIRS," found that when there are clear rules about how to handle conflict, men are much more willing to engage in conflict with women. This can work to everyone's benefit.

Before we buy into collective fictions that all men and all women are the same, or worse, that men and women are so different that they are incapable of ever meeting each other's needs, we need to remember that there is a wide range of variability. Sex roles are collectively held notions about behavior that describe aggregate phenomena, not individuals. This does not necessarily reflect what they are like in individual relationships, in which there can be tremendous variability.

Second-Half-of-Life-Issues

Half of the problems surrounding autonomy and commitment and the psychological issues they bring up for men and women are "stage phenomenon." They are related to identity issues men and women encounter in the first half of their lives and play out in their first marriages or serious relationships. What remains to be studied is whether the psychological dynamics of projection and control continue to exert the same power over men and women throughout life as they do in their twenties and early thirties. When men and women reach their mid-thirties and forties, it is likely that an entirely different set of psychological dynamics come into play. Once men and women have matured into a more grounded sense of who they are, the relational issues at mid-life have to do with sharing, raising the young, and contributing to society. Instead of dealing with pre-identity issues, at mid-life men and women begin to think about the mark they are going to leave, the loss of youth, and feelings about death.

The challenge of the 1990s, for men and women developing relationships during the mid-life phase, is to create a balance between similar and different psychological needs. The methods may be different, but men and women really want similar things from each other: intimacy, tenderness, caring, and sharing.

The collective theme emerging in the 1990s about behavior and relationships is relevant here. Family therapists such as Michael White talk about "co-constructing our reality" or "restorying our lives." We need to restory our *relationships* as we get ready to move into the 21st century. We need to discard antiquated notions about men and women being half people uniting into a whole, which the relationship encompasses. This is a dysfunctional version of being a couple; the relationship it creates is too rigid and one person always comes up short. We need a new definition of what keeps men and women together based on inter-relationship, not dependency.

CHAPTER SEVEN

Grown-Up Love for the Nineties

"....The best is yet to be;
The last of life, for which the first was made."

—Robert Browning

One of the advantages of the implicit pact that men and women made in the traditional 1950s style marriage was that everybody understood what their job was. From mowing the lawn to paying the bills to making the doctors' appointments for the children, the assignments were perfectly clear. There was no need to think about it or discuss it. Men earned the money and women took care of the house and the children. However, in the 1990s, with both men and women developing careers, and with many women formulating separate identities for themselves outside of their roles as wives and mothers, couples find themselves tailoring relationships to fit their needs. Many divide work responsibilities according to who has the time, the inclination, the willingness, and the ability to do a job, rather than just assigning chores on the basis of gender.

We talked to 15 career women in their thirties and forties to find out how their relationships work. All of the women were white, married (many for the second time), well-established professionals. Nine of the 15 were mothers, and two were the mothers of preschoolers. Two described their husbands as the one with primary responsibility for the children, while seven said they were the primary caretaker of the children, even if they also had hired help. Although none of the husbands said that they felt threatened by their wives' success, many of them said they still considered their own career to be the primary one in the family. Most of the husbands said that while they admired their wives' strength and independence, they were also attracted to the traditionally feminine side. Although most couples described a somewhat symmetrical or equal arrangement with their spouses, both in terms of financial and role responsibility, there was also a lingering legacy of the traditional complementary relationship, and some need to justify any of their role deviations from it.

Powerful Women, Weak Men?

A concern for both women and men is that if a woman is very successful in her career, she may intimidate men, or become so masculine that she will not be able to achieve a satisfactory relationship with a man. The 15 career women we interviewed occupied a continuum in terms of how traditional or non-traditional they were in their personal lives. Only two of the couples had fully reversed roles, where the wife was the primary wage-earner and the husband took care of the children. Two of the women considered themselves to be very traditional in their roles as wives and mothers, and others described ways in which they deviated from what they saw as normal traditional lifestyles. With the exception of one couple, all of them had entered their current relationship in a post-identity period of their lives, after the women had already established themselves professionally. With the exception of that one pre-identity marriage, all had been involved in previous relationships or marriages of varying lengths, and all had spent a significant period being alone. They described how they consciously looked for someone who was different from the person they were with in their previous relationships, and in making their current choice, how they had relied on compatibility of values, or personality traits, or some quality of friendship.

We asked them how they saw their relationships. Were their partners threatened by their success? We asked some of the men, as well, how they felt about their marriages to strong, independent women. We asked them to tell us about roles and power in their marriages and about how they solved problems.

There were a few common themes. The first was the importance of spending a significant period of time alone, before marrying. Another theme was that the women tended to view their own careers in a compartmentalized way; what happened at work was separate from what happened at home. Most of the women felt they were balancing their careers with their families, and some felt that they had been forced to make some compromises in terms of the time they spent with their children or with their spouses, or in career advancement.

Although we expected that most would say they had an egalitarian relationship, that was not true for all couples. Some were very traditional, while others were somewhere in the middle. Certainly the men participated in child-care and household chores more than the average man does (which is only between 1 and 1.8 hours per day, while working mothers do about 4.8 hours per day). For two couples, the discrepancy in earning abilities seemed to create some problems. Most of the relationships had some flexibility in role assignment, but half looked like traditional families in terms of the roles which the wife filled either in regards to her husband and the household or in terms of child-care.

How They Chose One Another

Many of the couples we talked to chose their spouses based on particular personality traits that they believed they wanted in a mate, and many of them had changed their criteria from what they looked for when they were younger. Marjorie was a junior high school teacher who spent most of her twenties dating good-looking jocks. "I wasn't really looking for a husband. I was just always looking for guys I was physically attracted to. There was a particular look I liked—like Nick Nolte, the blond Aryan. I was a physical education teacher so it was very important to me that the man be very physical."

In her mid-thirties, Marjorie decided that the men she had been dating were not good for her. "I had dated a lot of different guys who were really bad for me. I decided to change my criteria. I consciously thought about what I wanted in a husband, and I joined a video dating service. Like magic, my ideal man appeared in the catalog. I had seen him at a party and I liked him, and then the very next day I saw his picture at the dating service. It turned out that he had seen my video and had picked me, too. So it was a meant-to-be kind of thing."

The man Marjorie married was physically nothing like the men she previously had thought to be her type. "Ned doesn't fit any of that. He is bald and had a beard. There used to be a part of me that looked for someone who treated me poorly, and Ned treated me well and he didn't fool around with any manipulative games. He was straightforward from the get-go. I had liked to be held at bay and left worrying and wondering. I basically grew up."

Joan lived with a man from the time she was 25 until she was 34, and helped rear his three teen-aged sons. "It was a very dysfunctional relationship. I was not making very much money myself, and going to school part-time. He basically took care of me financially. As soon as I became financially independent, I was able to let go of him. It freed me up to find a person who accepted me as an independent person. Lyle doesn't lay any expectations on me."

Deciding What They Wanted

Among those who had been married before, many consciously looked for a different kind of person from their first spouse. They said they had learned something about the selection process the hard way.

Jessica, 34, a corporate attorney, said, "I met Steve eight months after my first husband and I separated. I consciously thought about wanting something very different. In fact, I told my first husband, I wouldn't even date you now...you know, the Porsche, the fancy fast cars, the parties, the bars. He had a glib personality. Those are the kinds of things I shied away from. I have observed among my colleagues that this kind of guy, the handsome, slick guy with the fast car, is the kind who is likely to be cheating on his wife. I wanted a man who wanted to get married, to have children, whose values of life were for a modest financial lifestyle, who wanted to spend time with the family instead of providing them with a lot of money. I wanted somebody honest. I had no tolerance for the remotely slippery, sneaky kind of a mystery man. My first husband always had an air of mystery. That was very appealing to me when I was in college, but now I wanted a man who was stable, honest, and natural, with no dark corners."

Joanne was working on the stage crew for a theater company when she met Ted, an actor. She had been living with someone for eight years, but Ted kept asking her out for dinner, and finally she accepted. "I knew I wanted someone who could communicate, who was more verbal, who wanted to share thoughts and feelings. Probably I was looking for something more romantic. I needed a more romantic human being. Ted is a real verbal person, a vulnerable person, a real communicator. I think I was what he was looking for—a strong woman and a nice woman. He never said that but it was pretty clear."

Laurene, a psychologist, said, "I used to be sexually attracted to people who subconsciously reminded me of people I was used to in my family. I was picking people who were always mad at me, or who always thought I had done something wrong, or men who were emotionally unavailable to me because they were preoccupied with their own issues. I had a major pattern-interrupt when I decided to stop dating men to whom I was sexually attracted. I actually started turning men down saying, 'I'm attracted to you, so obviously you are no good for me.'"

When she first met Frank, the owner of a chain of retail stores, she thought of him as just a friend. "Then I started to look at what he was. He wasn't boring. He was a really good man. I wasn't incredibly sexually attracted to him at first, but now we have incredible sexual chemistry. He has everything I ever looked for. He was absolutely committed to me. There were no games. He didn't play it cool. He came after me like there was no other goal in the world worth pursuing. I liked his consistency. I told him I was afraid he would get scared and run, and he said, 'Not me, babe. I can take as much closeness as you can give, and still want more.'"

Steve can't even remember what he was looking for in a wife when he met and married for the first time, right out of college.

"But after being divorced, I wanted a woman like Jessica. I felt I wanted somebody normal, down-to-earth, level-headed."

Steve said that during the time he was single, he felt that most of the women he met had been damaged and were extremely distrustful of men. "I felt like I had to suffer the consequences of all the experiences of inequality of women in the world, that somehow I had to take the brunt of such extremes." Steve said his first wife had difficulty reconciling her roles as wife and career woman. "Her profession was the first priority and marriage was second, and she said that. She made that very clear. For instance, if we had a baby in my first marriage, I would have had to stay home and raise it. All the roles would have had to be reversed in order to compensate for her feelings of what it is like to be a woman in the 1990s."

In his second marriage, he said, "I wanted someone much more nurturing and loving and down-to-earth, with no games being played. I wanted to feel as though we were both on equal footing." Steve says that Jessica "doesn't feel like she has to make her mark on the world and I have to be part of the slash-and-burn wasteland left behind. She's willing to treat me as an equal, and as a friend, and as a husband."

Choosing A Friend

Others we talked to echoed the theme that they had married a person who was first and foremost a friend.

"We were best friends for eight years before we got married," Mike, a music composer, said. "I think that marriage should be like friendship, with sex added."

Joe, a psychotherapist, said, "I was feeling distrustful of women after my previous marriage ended and I really didn't want to get involved, but Margaret was very comfortable to be with. I was not feeling like I had to compromise who I was for the sake of the relationship. The relationship was going just fine. When it finally sank in that life was really comfortable with this woman and we were great companions, I started to take the idea seriously that we could be companions for life."

"I feel like with Margaret I've come home. I don't have to compromise who I am. There were so many things that just meshed. She had been thinking about converting to Judaism before she ever even met me. The first ring she tried on when we got engaged was perfect, the first wedding dress she tried on was the one she bought. It was like everything all fell into place without resistance, that things just happened so wonderfully."

Marjorie said her meeting with her husband was "a meant-to-be kind of thing."

Joan says that Lyle "was a very sensitive man. He cared about being friends, not just lovers."

The Importance of Being Alone

Both the men and women we talked to mentioned that they felt that it had been important for them to spend a period of their lives alone before entering into this significant relationship. They said this period had been instrumental in helping them reassess themselves and their life goals, and in altering their abilities to trust themselves and to handle intimacy.

"In my twenties, I was not as evolved. At 22, I was still in the role that I felt I needed a man to take care of me. It was not something I had been taught by my parents, but just something that the society around me had foisted upon me," said Jean, 59, who met Arthur, 60, when both of them were in college, but didn't marry him until she met him again a quarter of a century later.

"This time in my life, I didn't need anyone to look after me. I was perfectly able to take care of myself," she said.

The circumstances of Jean's and Arthur's lives are radically different from the other couples we interviewed. As a child, Jean had survived a Nazi concentration camp, and that experience, she said, had made her so distrustful that she rejected Arthur when they first met in their twenties. Their love, however, survived for more than two decades, while each was married to someone else. After they were both divorced they met again in their forties. The intermediary period alone, Jean says, contributed to her grounded sense of self. She had evolved into a whole person, who was able to let Arthur in. She felt that being secure within herself first was very significant in enabling her to trust Arthur to be her husband. Jean's issues of trust were extreme, but her feelings of self-trust were not unlike those expressed by other women.

Andrea, 52, who was separated from her husband of 28 years, said that the separation had helped them see each other as individuals. "We were so co-dependent I never needed to see that he could take care of himself and survive without me. I needed to learn to take care of me first. I've always taken care of everyone else first," she said.

Joe said he felt that one of the reasons he and Margaret were ready for each other when they met was that both had been single for a long period of time, "and we had gotten singleness out of our systems. We were past the stage of needing that addictive, chemical kind of love. My past relationships had really taught me a great deal about what I wanted."

Are Men Threatened By Strong Women?

"Powerful women...are far more interesting and exciting, and that makes for much more of a passionate relationship," said Steve, a 35-year-old art dealer.

Joan, a sales executive who earned almost twice as much as her therapist husband, said that Lyle "takes pride in me and my job. He brags about me. He pumps me up. There's no resentment that I earn more."

Laurene says that Frank "was not intimidated by me at all. He looked at me and said, 'I like it that you are a strong, independent career woman type.'"

The men interviewed acknowledged that their wives were competent and aggressive in the outside world, but said that they were also attracted to them because of their capacity to disclose their more vulnerable, feminine side to their mates.

"As an attorney, she has to be extremely aggressive, but she has found an ability to use that aggression at work and leave it at work and not bring it home with her, which I've found to be very wonderful," Steve said.

The men saw the women as balanced. They were attracted to both the strong and the vulnerable sides.

Arthur says, "Other people see Jean as the strong one, but there are sides to her that people don't see and that she doesn't allow them to see. I look after that side. I look after her because she has been hurt a lot in life. I take care of the scared part of her."

Laurene says that Frank sees "both sides of me. He sees the competent woman and the scared little girl who doesn't know what she is doing. And I thought I was hiding that part so well."

Some of the women chose to play down their professionalism and accentuate their more traditional feminine sides in their personal relationships.

Barbara, 46, a doctor married to an insurance salesman for the past 22 years, claimed she didn't know whether she made more money than he did. "Oh I don't know," she shrugged. "He does all the bookkeeping and the tax returns. I probably do have a higher gross, but my overhead is so much higher... I really don't know."

Egalitarian Values Around Roles

In a more symmetrical relationship, couples have more flexibility in who takes on which job. For the most part, the husbands we spoke to were very interested in their children and in participating in child-care. Most of the husbands took some responsibility for housework, too. In some cases, however, the roles actually were reversed.

Steve and Jessica share household chores. "I always insist, half-jokingly, that if one person cooks, the other one does the dishes, but in reality, even when I cook I usually do the dishes. She has to fight me for it. I'm fairly anal-retentive, so I'm usually the one who keeps things clean around the house," he said. Steve and Jessica were expecting their first child, and Jessica felt some conflict about going back to work when her three-month maternity leave ended. Steve said, "I certainly want to try to make every effort to share responsibility as much as possible. That's very important to me personally, but I realize that some of those things are not as easily shared as others, in terms of the mother versus the father roles. But it is important for me to try to do as much as possible as far as things I am capable of doing."

Mike and his wife also share household chores, although he said that sometimes when he gets tired, "I do get this irrational tingle that my father didn't have to do this."

He said, "It is my job just as much as it is hers to carry half the load of the family. Sometimes it is my male instinct to resent that. But she is my friend, and this is a partnership."

Mike said when their first child was born, "there was an incredible amount of turmoil and a lot of anger and frustration. No one is ever prepared for what it is going to be like to have a baby and to have so much responsibility and so much sleep deprivation."

Mike said he spends more time with their five-year-old daughter than his wife does, but she is the one who keeps track of when the doctors' appointments are and oversees the child's needs. They also have hired help to watch their daughter when they both work.

Joanne, a television producer, and her husband Ted, an actor, have been married for 17 years and have a five-year-old daughter. "Ted takes a lot of responsibility for her because he works less than I do," Joanne says. "He picks her up from school and he is the primary parent. We share everything else."

Jessica said, "It was all right with Steve that I didn't like to cook, and all right that I wanted to keep the finances separate, and all right that I worked and was successful."

Although many couples share roles, the mothers were more likely to take on fairly traditional roles.

Carol gave up her private practice of medicine and went into a group practice because it gave her more flexibility to care for her four children. Although her husband helps with carpooling, she called him otherwise "very non-involved, and that causes us some stress."

How They Resolve Conflicts

Joe, a psychotherapist, said that he and his saleswoman wife Margaret "don't store up resentments. When an issue comes up we talk things out and reaffirm our commitment. It gets aired. Both of us would rather be clear with each other."

Steve said he is less aggressive and confrontational than his attorney wife, "and sometimes she'll say, 'You need to stand your ground and fight back. It's annoying when you don't fight back and I'm going to respect you more if you do'... If I feel strongly enough I will take a stand. Most of the time I don't feel pushed around, so I don't say anything. It's not in my nature, but if something really bothers me, I speak up, and she says, 'Gee, you really can speak your mind and be opinionated on certain subjects.'"

Joanne said, "Sometimes we are able to handle conflict and sometimes we aren't. We bash away at issues... usually good-humoredly. We've been in couples therapy and we've brought issues in there. Usually it is the small stuff that we fight over. The big stuff we agree on."

Mike said, "We still flare up sometimes and get alienated, but we love each other and there is a lot of mutual respect. We're not children and we've known each other a long time. I can get a little ego thing sometimes. When I'm wrong, I know it instantly, but it's hard for me to go in and apologize for what I've said. She is more traditionally feminine. Women don't seem to be as interested in winning as in resolving conflict."

Love in a Time of Transition

The problems mentioned by the couples we spoke to centered around task overload, work commitments that prevented the women from staying home and spending as much time with their children as they desired, and uneasiness about how to handle their new roles. Some pointed out ways that their marriages differed from ones in the storybooks.

Creating a new kind of relationship does not occur without conflict. The 1990s are clearly a transitional time, with couples who have grown up accepting basic premises of feminism attempting to put them into action in their own marriages. The children of these couples will grow up with very different role models than their own parents had. Little boys who have seen their fathers cooking and their mothers going off to the office will have different notions about what is normal when they make matches of their own. But these are transitional relationships.

Throughout their 17 year marriage, Joanne has worked more steadily than Ted, although both have had ups and downs.

"He does mind that I make more, not because I am making more money, but because he would like to be making a fortune himself. He'd like to be more successful than he is."

Joan said that Lyle doesn't mind the fact that she earns more than he does, but sometimes it bothers her. "He gets nervous thinking about being in the sole provider role, but I wish he were making more."

Some Traditional Residuals

Particularly when it comes to children, most of the couples expressed some longing for more traditional roles. Problems sometimes arise when couples confront new roles that once again trigger their unconscious template of how roles are supposed to be. Couples who have managed to be egalitarian in their roles as husband and wife face new challenges with parenthood.

Jessica says, "It is very nice that Steve wants to take paternity leave and stay home with the baby, but I want to stay home, too. I think we may be entering into a no-man's land. Some of the other women at my office have had babies and one or two came back to work after six weeks, leaving the baby with a live-in nurse. I don't know if I can do that."

Margaret echoed her ambivalence. "It'll tear me apart to have to work when we have a baby," she said. "I'd like to have two or three years off for a simple life with my child, and I do picture myself eventually going back into the workforce, but my more practical side says it isn't a good time to leave the workforce and assume you will be able to go back. But I am ready to stay home and do babytalk."

Joanne said, "It was a huge conflict for me when I first went back to work after the baby was born. I kept thinking, 'What am I doing? What am I taking away from myself and my child?' But I found out that someone else [namely, her husband] could do it. So that took away some of the guilt. But at work, when someone is just taking up my time, I tend not to want to put up with them, because I've got more important things waiting for me at home."

Postponed Marriage

Women who remain single during their twenties and into their thirties before finding a life mate experience different circumstances than women who live under their father's roofs until he escorts them down the aisle and turns them over to another male protector. Women who wait to marry, or who marry young, divorce, and consider marrying again later in life, have not held their identities in abeyance waiting to find a man to complete them. These woman have separate identities of their own. They don't need a man to give them a sense of who they are. Among the women who wait to marry until later in life, some still cling to the traditional values they learned in childhood, and wish to maintain a traditional complementary style marriage where the husband is, if not the sole wage-earner, the primary one. Many women, even those who enjoy their work and take pride in it, still prefer to give priority to their husband's job over theirs.

"We both value the career that I have," Joe said. "She makes a great deal of money at her job, and she is good at what she does, but overall she values what I do and respects my work more than hers. I think she sees my work as more important to society than her work. Our shared perception is that my work is of greater value."

And Mike, who writes songs, said, "We're not mercenary, but I think we both recognize that the way we're going to get where we're going is through me. My career takes precedence sometimes."

Mature Love: Being Separate Together

Psychologists Otto Kernberg and Martin Bergman wrote in 1976 that love produces a "normal idealization" of the partner. In other words, lovers see each other as representing the best of everything, both in terms of cultural standards and of their own personal standards. There is a feeling that they are special as a pair. In terms of sexuality, mature love is characterized by the desire to give pleasure to the partner as well as to get pleasure oneself.

A central characteristic of mature love is the ability to tolerate differences, since each is separate within the pair. Kernberg says that the combination of wanting to be together, while rejecting fusion, adds depth and complexity to mature relationships.

Jean and Arthur say that one of the strengths of their marriage is that they have been able to maintain separate interests and friends without it threatening the relationship. Jean has a close male friend whom Arthur dislikes. "I say, I know you don't like him, so maybe we can spend some time together, and then I'll spend some time alone with him? And it will be all right with Arthur. I can spend time with my friends and my husband doesn't mind. By the same token, it feels all right to me that he has a separate life that does not always include me." Both Jean and Arthur had learned to trust themselves in the period of time they spent alone.

The Individualized Marriage Contract

Once a woman has formed an identity of her own, what she needs in marriage changes from someone to complete her to someone to share her life with. When we talked to couples who met and married in their thirties and forties, the theme of partnership was evident. They described it in different ways, but the predominant theme was that they wanted to be on more equal footing in terms of power and control.

They had more flexibility in creating the rules and the roles that they were to adopt in the relationship. The issue of children, rather than being a given, was something to be negotiated: whether or not they wanted to have children, or, in cases where there were already children from previous liaisons, how these children would be included in their lives.

The parenting role, rather than being unilaterally assigned to the wife, was shared in part by the husband. In two instances, the husbands took the larger role. For some couples, this was a point of contention, and they were not really comfortable with their present resolution. Others who chose to have children found it difficult to adjust to playing their parental roles in a different manner than their parents did when they were growing up. Some women who enjoyed their careers found that when they were faced with motherhood it was wrenching to think of working all day and leaving the bulk of the child-care to someone else. Because they had stay-at-home mothers, they felt guilty if they didn't mother in the same manner.

New Roles and Shared Assumptions

One clear theme among the couples we talked to was the need to accept some kind of compromise. No matter how they had fantasized about how their relationship or their household would be managed, all had faced the necessity of compromising to establish new roles in the face of outdated stereotypes, age-old demands, and changing expectations. While accepting the compromise, they also needed to accept the fact that there would be conflict stemming from a sudden shift in cultural and familial values.

It takes 30 years to alter values on a collective level, according to futurists. Everyone with whom we spoke talked about how their marriage and lifestyle differed from those of their parents and even from their notion of what marriage was supposed to be. They weren't necessarily making a judgment about which was better, but they were aware of the differences.

CHAPTER EIGHT

Planning a Strategy

$\mathcal{T}$here's an old saying that you find happiness when you aren't looking for it. To turn the search for a life partner into a single-minded crusade is a mistake. Instead of looking for a man, think about how you can extend your horizons, enlarge your social circle, and make your life more interesting. The more people you know— men and women, married and single, old and young—the more chances you have of meeting Mr. Right. One thing is sure, how-ever; he's unlikely to ride up in front of your apartment building on a white steed if you spend all your evenings alone at home in front of the television set.

Conversely, if you spend all your evenings attending one singles event after another, looking for a man, you are likely to acquire the aura of a desperate woman, which is the ultimate turn-off to a man. Singles events have their place, but they should only be one part of your strategy, not the whole plot.

Winning and Losing Attitudes

What separates winners from losers in any endeavor is persistence and stamina. Losers give up when they don't get what they want immediately. Some women join a video dating service, and if the first ten men they pick don't choose them, they quit. Or they go to a singles dance, and if they don't see someone they find attractive within the first 15 minutes, they go home. That's being a loser. A winner says, "So what if the first ten men rejected me? There are 200 other attractive men in these files." A winner knows that finding the right man is a numbers game, and that the more men you meet, the greater the chance is of finding one with whom you click.

Donna, 32, was afraid of attending singles events or joining groups where she might meet men, for fear of being rejected. "I'd feel like such a jerk," she said, "if I got all dressed up and went there and I didn't meet anyone. If nobody asked me for my number, I'd feel like a failure."

A friend of hers bet Donna that she couldn't get rejected six times in one evening.

"Go to a singles dance, and ask different men to dance until you've been turned down by six of them," the friend challenged her.

So Donna took the challenge.

She discovered that men almost never say no when a woman asks them to dance. Occasionally they will, but it is almost impossible to be rejected repeatedly during the course of an evening. And, of course, trying to be rejected in order to win the bet removed the stigma from it. What Donna learned from the evening was that she really didn't get rejected very often, and when she did, it wasn't fatal. So many men accepted her advances that her self-esteem was bolstered rather than diminished.

The foundation for a winning attitude is a good sense of self-esteem. On the NBC television sit-com, "Golden Girls," the character Blanche (played by actress Rue McClanahan) is a femme fatale who never has any trouble attracting a man. On one episode, Blanche confides to Dorothy (played by Bea Arthur) that when she feels self-confidence slipping, she makes a list of her three best qualities and repeats them to herself.

"My name is Blanche Devereaux. I'm beautiful, men find me attractive, and everybody likes me." She advises Dorothy to do the same thing.

Dorothy says, "I'm beautiful, men find me attractive and everybody likes me."

"No, no, no," Blanche laughs. "I didn't mean to confuse you. You need to say things that apply to you... like you're a good speller and you're always prompt." Blanche ponders for a moment, trying to think of another adjective to describe Dorothy, and finally says, "Well, there's no law that says you have to name three."

The scene is comedy, of course, but as Freud said, things are funny when there is truth behind the humor. It does help to remind yourself of your good qualities, and that if you like yourself, other people will like you too.

Everyone has good qualities. We've all known women who weren't particularly attractive physically, who still were popular with men and women alike. You don't have to be classically beautiful for one man to find you beautiful. If you have a pleasing personality, many people will be attracted to you, no matter what you look like.

While it helps to have a good figure, being overweight doesn't mean that you can't find a man. It is true there are some men who would never date a woman who hasn't got a perfect figure, but there are plenty of other men who will. Indeed, there are men who far prefer heavy, or tall, or otherwise outside-the-norm-women.

Being outside the norm narrows your odds, but hardly eliminates them.

Polly's husband left her when she was 41, after 18 years of marriage. Although she had been slender as a bride, over the years her weight had yo-yoed, and at the time of the divorce, she was nearly 50 pounds overweight—far more than pleasingly plump. The fact that her husband had left her had devastated her self-esteem, and she was afraid that her extra pounds would mean that no other man would look at her. But a friend who had been divorced and on the singles scene for several years advised her to go to a singles dance and "practice" flirting.

"Just get dressed up and go," her friend urged her. "You won't necessarily meet anyone special. Just see what it is like. You've been off the market for so long, you've forgotten what it's like to flirt, so just go and look around and see what it feels like. Consider it an investigation."

Filled with trepidation, but determined to get on with her life, Polly went to the dance by herself. (Although going with another woman may make you feel more secure, men find it more difficult to approach several women standing together than a woman standing by herself.) She drove her own car, and carried a small purse containing only enough cash for the evening, her lipstick, and her car keys, so she wouldn't feel uncomfortable putting it down on a table if someone asked her to dance.

When she first walked in, she bought herself a drink and sat down to watch what was going on. In only a few minutes, she observed that men seldom approached a woman who was seated. It was easier to cruise by a woman who was standing, and if she was interested, she made eye contact and smiled. If she wasn't, she looked away, and he walked on by. If a woman made eye contact with the man—thus giving him permission to approach her—and if he also found her within acceptable parameters, he would stop and initiate a conversation, usually asking her to dance.

After a few minutes, Polly got up and stood near the dance floor, ostensibly watching the dancers, but also in a traffic pattern where people walked by her to get to the bar. She quickly discovered that if she made eye contact with men passing her, almost all of them would at least say "hi," to her, and that most would stop to talk. If she found a man unattractive, the simplest thing to do was to avert her gaze as he passed, so as not to grant him permission to approach her. After a few minutes, a man asked her to dance. They wound up spending most of the evening talking together. Although this encounter did not lead to a long-term relationship, it broke the ice for Polly, proving to her that there were indeed men who would find her attractive, despite her excess weight.

Over the next few months, as she became initiated into the dating scene, she discovered that while there were probably many men who automatically ruled her out because of her weight, those men did not interact with her at all, so she never felt insulted or rejected by them. What's more, she wasn't interested in them and their values. At every event where there were single men, there was a sufficient number of men who found her attractive and interesting. Because of her weight problem, she found that she could avoid rejection by waiting to see which men approached her, rather than by approaching men herself. But on evenings when she was feeling particularly self-confident, she would select a man she found attractive and walk up and ask him to dance.

"Men almost never turn a woman down when she asks them to dance," she said. "And all it obligates them to do is spend a few minutes together on the dance floor. If they don't find me attractive, they can walk away after the dance ends. But during the few minutes while we are dancing, I talk to them, and if they like my personality, they stay with me."

Polly also made it a rule to always accept when a man asked her to dance, even if she was not especially attracted by his appearance. Sometimes after a few minutes of conversation, she found that he was more interesting than she thought. But even if she wasn't interested in him, just by accepting his invitation and getting out on the dance floor with him, she signaled to the other men in the room that she was a friendly, approachable woman. "If she'll dance with him, maybe she'll dance with me," they might think. A surprising number of women attend singles events, and then refuse to dance with the men who ask them. Even etiquette books will tell you that's bad manners, and besides, you are committing yourself to only a few minutes on the dance floor.

Risking

Some women reject men out-of-hand because they don't like their looks. They are holding out for their fantasy man, and this protects them from being rejected. They think, "I don't have to risk anything because he is not really good enough." The psychological game they play is that only one of them is okay. Either they're okay and he's not, or he's okay, and they're not. They are too afraid of rejection to accept the fact that both of them are okay.

If the fact that someone to whom you are attracted does not find you equally attractive causes you to conclude that something must be wrong with you, then you will be afraid to take the risk of wanting him at all. In order to protect yourself from the possibility of being rejected, you would rather sit home and not put yourself in a position where anyone could reject you. The by-product is that at the same time, you have placed yourself in a position where nobody can accept you either, so your fear that no one wants you is reinforced.

The way to overcome the fear of rejection is to reframe it, or change its meaning. Instead of thinking that there is something wrong with you because a particular man you find attractive does not reciprocate your feelings, think to yourself that he is simply not ready for a relationship, or that you want different things out of life, or that you have different values. If you see yourself as a worthwhile person, then you can recognize that your interest in him is a compliment to him. If he doesn't return the compliment, you will survive. Treat it as though he had said, "No thank you, I don't feel like accepting tonight." The key is to change from "I'm okay and he's not," or "He's okay and I'm not," to "He's okay and I'm okay too." The rejection is merely situational. There are a number of valid reasons why a man might reject you.

- He might be involved with someone else.
- He might not be ready for a relationship.
- He might be having a bad day.
- You may have different goals or values or lack complementary psychological needs.

Never make the generalization in your mind that because one man said no, all men will say no. There is always someone out there who will love you the way you are, if you love yourself, and if you take the time to care about him.

Beginning to Move Out

Step One

Increase your consciousness about what you are looking for in a mate. As long as you make all of your decisions based on chemical attraction or unconscious psychological needs, without thinking about what kind of man is good for you, you will continue to play out the old scripts with their old unhappy endings. Formulate a list of criteria of what you are looking for in a mate: personality traits, compatible pastimes, appropriate life stage, and shared values.

Step Two

Develop your sense of self-esteem. You have to like yourself first before you can expect that someone else will like you. Make a list of your own good attributes and turn them into a list of affirmations that you can repeat to yourself when you are feeling low. You want to make a list of qualities about yourself that are worthwhile, and a list of things that you do well. Affirmations about your own good qualities are called "being strokes," and the ones about things you do well are "doing strokes." A "being stroke" is "I am kind and intelligent and considerate of others." Your "doing stroke" might be "I am a good cook, a good skier, and a good dancer." By giving yourself positive strokes, you invalidate that little voice in you which is always lurking, ready to come out and tell you that you're not worthwhile. Most people spend more time giving themselves negative strokes, thinking to themselves, "I'm fat," or "I'm too old." Reverse that by giving yourself positive strokes every day.

Sandra, 32, an executive secretary, signed up to take part in a singles gourmet club. At the first meeting, she approached an attractive man and tried to start a conversation. He was curt with her and walked away. In the past, Sandra would have used his unfriendliness as a statement about her own self-worth, and she would have thought, "Oh, there is something wrong with me. He doesn't like me." But instead she said to herself, "I wonder why this guy bothered to come to this dinner party, if he wasn't interested in being friendly. There must be something wrong with him today. I'll go talk to someone else." So she approached another man, and he asked her out for the next Saturday night.

When You Still Feel Bad

For many women, negative thought habits run deep—so deep, and so seemingly invisible, that you are only aware of persistent negative feelings. The first step in overcoming negative thoughts about yourself is to recognize that you have them. Then you need to take control of the negative complex. Think of the complex as being separate from yourself, as being an entity of its own. You aren't the one who is criticizing yourself—that evil twin is the one who is doing it. You can de-identify with the complex by giving it a name of its own. When you start to think something bad about yourself, like, "How stupid of me. I am always so clumsy," immediately correct yourself by thinking to yourself, "Oh, there goes that evil witch saying bad things about me again."

The steps to go through are:
1. Recognize that your negative thoughts are a complex.
2. Name the complex and give it an identity separate from yourself.
3. Separate from the complex by talking to it through dialogue, letter, clay, or art. Quiet that inner voice.
4. Replace the negative feelings with positive affirmations.

The goal is to separate the complex from your ego. By naming it, you cease to see it as a symbol of your entire self. It becomes just an aspect. You stop identifying with it.

What is it that triggers those negative thoughts? For many women, what triggers a negative complex is rejection. They ask someone to come for dinner, and they are turned down. Instead of thinking, "Well, they have other plans," the woman thinks to herself, "They don't like me. There's something wrong with me. I'm not okay."

The thing to do at this point is to immediately think, "There's that voice again, telling me I'm not all right." Then remind yourself of your positive attributes. "Of course I'm all right. I'm pretty and intelligent and fun to be with. They'd be lucky to come to my house and spend an evening with me because I make great pasta and I'm witty and amusing."

When you feel good about yourself, you project, you smile, you radiate good vibes, and both men and women respond positively to you. Thinking highly of yourself turns you into an internal "10." Men and women alike are as attracted to internal 10s as external 10s. That may be why men flock around some women who aren't pretty at all and shy away from some who look like Miss America.

Maintaining Your Femininity

Another aspect of winning at the dating game is maintaining some aspects of traditional femininity. Some women who are successful in the business world find it difficult to operate in a relational context outside of the office.

Playing the ultimate career woman in the film "All About Eve," Bette Davis says that as they climb the corporate ladder, women forget how to be women, and that sooner or later, they need to regain their femininity.

In her 1988 book *Being a Woman*, former radio psychologist Dr. Toni Grant says that "Getting married does not so much demand that a woman do something, but rather that she be in the right frame of mind for bonding with a man. This frame of mind can be characterized as a uniquely feminine attitude, a particular way of being a woman. But the modern woman has denounced and suppressed this way of being in the world and now needs to be encouraged to embrace her lost femininity...."

Women who are able to be aggressive in their professional lives, and to achieve balance between their masculine and feminine sides in their personal lives, believe they have the best of both worlds.

The attributes that make a woman successful in the work world are diametrically opposed to those that epitomize femininity. A career woman would be described as very adult, with good cognitive skills, in control of her emotions, and strong in negotiation skills. In short, she has a strong ego. A feminine woman would be described as receptive, other-directed, a good caretaker, nurturer, and manager.

Some women experience a strong internal conflict between the need to be one way in the work world and another way in their relationships. They haven't forgotten what they learned while they were growing up about how to be a woman, but they can't reconcile it with the skills they need to succeed in the business world. Mother said that girls let the boys win. But that doesn't work in the business world. Feeling unable to play by two sets of rules, some women withdraw from the race.

What's Behind Being Too Picky?

Some women who aren't ready for a relationship, or who are too afraid to be intimate, protect themselves by being overly picky.

In *Games People Play*, transactional analyst Eric Berne defined a psychological game as a transaction between two human beings which seems simple and direct, but has an underlying and sometimes unconscious hidden agenda. Berne describes a game called "Blemish," in which the partners avoid intimacy by finding fault with each other.

Women who find something wrong with every man who shows an interest in them—"He's a sweet guy, but he's too short," or "I'm crazy about him, but he doesn't earn as much money as I do," are playing the Blemish game. Since no man is ever quite right, they avoid facing their own fear of intimacy or the conflicts it may entail for them.

Martha, 38, a Harvard MBA, attended her 20-year high school reunion and told an old friend that she was afraid she was never going to get married because she never met any suitable men.

"Why don't you take up golf?" her friend suggested.

"I don't like men who play golf," Martha retorted.

That's being too picky. Martha rejected categorically all men who play golf, without seeing what they looked like, what they did for a living, or what their personalities were like. Needless to say, not all men who play golf are alike.

Louise, 39, joined a video dating service and reported that all the men she met through it were crazy or were intimidated by an intelligent woman. In order to mask her own internal conflicts, Louise was being too picky. She was the one with the problem, not the men she was meeting. She was afraid of being rejected, so she did the rejecting first.

Plenty of women meet men who aren't crazy through dating services. If Louise meets only the crazy ones, either there's something wrong with the way she presents herself or with the way she selects them. Most men like intelligent women, and if Louise can't find any, she's probably the one doing something wrong. Since she's an aggressive career woman with strong masculine qualities, to find a man who is complementary to her, the 50s model her mother would love, she would have to find a man with a strong feminine side. However, she's too critical of these men who are attracted to her. She needs to look at how being overly critical serves to protect her.

The Divorced Person's Trap

People who have been divorced, especially, must work through the emotional baggage from the failed relationship before they are ready to enter into another serious relationship. The book *Second Chances*, by Judith S. Wallerstein and Sandra Blakeslee, examines the effect of divorce on husbands, wives, and children in the decade following the marital separation and concludes that divorce is a profoundly life-changing event for everyone concerned, and that it produces clear winners and losers.

Contrary to the widespread belief that most people get over the trauma of divorce within a year or so, Wallerstein and Blakeslee found that it took women an average of three to three and a half years and men two to two-and-a-half years to regain a sense of equilibrium after their separation.

They found that even ten years after their divorce, almost half of the women and two-thirds of the men they studied said the quality of their lives was no better than before the divorce.

"Recovery is not a given in adult life," Wallerstein and Blakeslee wrote. "The assumption that all people recover psychologically is not based on evidence. On what basis do we make the assumption that after 20 or 25 years of marriage people can inevitably pick themselves back up and start over again?

"Feelings, especially angry feelings and feelings of hurt and humiliation, can remain in full force for many years after divorce."

Just because you're single—or divorced—doesn't mean you are ready for a new relationship. To be emotionally ready and open for a new and meaningful relationship, you have to have finished emotionally with the old one.

Kelly, who had been married to Stuart for 25 years, was an inveterate matchmaker. She had managed to fix up nearly all her friends with the men they later married. When she met Joel, a 44-year-old divorced man at a party, she figured he would be perfect for her friend, Julie, a school teacher who had been divorced for 14 years. Julie was a petite brunette with a biting wit, and Kelly thought Joel, who was a stand-up comedian, would like her. They shared the same religion, they lived in the same part of town, and they were both in the same socio-economic bracket. Kelly gave Joel Julie's number and he called and asked her to dinner.

The morning after the date, Joel told Kelly, "Julie is very pretty and very nice, but I don't think she's ready to date yet."

"What do you mean?" Kelly asked. "She's been divorced for 14 years."

"That's what I mean," Joel said. "She's not ready. She's been divorced for 14 years and that was all she could talk about."

One of Wallerstein and Blakeslee's most surprising findings was that young men whose first marriages ended while they were in their twenties seemed lost and rudderless as they moved into their thirties. They theorized that the divorce blocked them from moving through their normal life tasks as husbands and fathers during that decade of their lives.

Wallerstein and Blakeslee also found that where spouses had affairs before the divorce, it had a devastating effect on their partners' self-esteem that took years to overcome.

While divorce is distressing to both parties, probably the one who decided to leave the marriage is able to recover from it sooner than the one who was left. (In Wallerstein and Blakeslee's study, 100 percent of the men who initiated the separation did so only when they had another woman waiting in the wings.) For those who have not put the divorce to rest, and recovered from the pain, disappointment, or sense of failure, these issues block their ability to go out and risk again.

Readiness for widows and widowers is another story. In order to be ready, they need to have dealt with their grief and put the past behind them. They usually have not had the blow to their self-esteem suffered by those whose partners chose to leave them.

Chance Encounters

Many people believe that finding true love is a matter of chance encounters. It's all in the timing, they say. You have to be ready. There is certainly wisdom in that, since if you weren't ready, you wouldn't recognize Mr. Right if he hit you with a two-by-four. In the movies, most people seem to meet by chance—"cute meets" where boy bumps into girl and causes her to drop all of her packages, or when he stops to help her change a flat tire. In real life, you can increase your chances of an encounter by going to more places and meeting more people.

Reframing Your Search

The best place to meet a man is *everywhere*. Finding the right person is not a question of where you are, but how you are. If you have the right mindset, act friendly, feel good about yourself, and *are able to take risks*, any place is the right place. Instead of looking for a potential mate, reframe your search to encompass enlarging your social circle. Start thinking of ways to meet new and interesting people of both sexes. One of the best ways to meet a good man is to be introduced by another friend, so the more people you know, the better your chances are of meeting the right guy.

Instead of seeing every person you talk to as a potential date, your goal *should be* simply expanding your circle of acquaintances. Everyone you meet has a circle of approximately 30 people, which translates to many more new people to meet. Most people love to introduce someone they like to their friends. So, if you meet someone you like, chances are they will have friends that you would also find interesting. Your job is to be friendly, attractive, supportive, and interesting. If your conversation leads either of you to ask for a date or suggest another rendezvous, that's terrific. To protect yourself from disappointments, reframe your goal to just meeting more people.

Waiting in Lines

As long as you are going to wait in line...

- at the supermarket
- at the hardware store
- at the post office
- at the airport, train station, bus or ferry terminal
- on the ski slopes
- at the video store

...you might as well stand in line next to the most attractive man or woman and practice your conversational skills. You'll have a captive audience for the next few minutes. In the check-out line in the supermarket, or while waiting for cold cuts at a delicatessen, you can strike up a conversation without appearing to be overly aggressive. If he doesn't like you, he won't enter into the conversation. If he does, he may pursue it.

Hardware and discount home supply stores are fertile places to meet men, particularly if you need some advice about a plumbing leak or the best brand of paint.

Taking Chances in the Right Places

Men are everywhere. You need to put yourself in places where you have enough time to start a conversation.

Exercise One:

Step One: Find out from a clerk in your supermarket what time single men shop at the store. (Many men shop after work on a Monday or Tuesday night. In your area it may be Saturday morning, but the clerks at the store will know.)

Step Two: Shop at your market at the time the clerk suggests and follow the most interesting man you see into line.

Step Three: Start a conversation with him (you can always use something in his basket as a cue, or a headline on one of the tabloid newspapers on the checkout stand racks as an opening line).

Exercise Two

Go to your local hardware store, post office, etc. on a Saturday morning and, while waiting in line, start a conversation with a man in front of or behind you.

Exercise Three

A funny thing happens to people when they travel; they tend to talk more openly to strangers. If you are traveling alone (which really is the best way to travel for meeting men), you can ask the airline attendant at the desk to seat you next to a man who's traveling alone. You'll have a captive audience, and what else are you going to do on the plane? Read a book? You can do that at home.

Exercise Four

Find an attractive man who appears to be traveling alone. Ask him if he would mind watching your bags for a few moments. You now have a great introductory set-up. All you have to do is smile and ask where he's going.

If the thought of doing these exercises makes your heart race and your palms sweat, it's probably because you think that these "forward" maneuvers won't be a success unless he asks you out, or you ask him. Just think of it as practice. You don't have to follow up at all, but it is a good idea to get the man's card, so that if you would like to call him again, you can.

If you concentrate on finding more activities to get involved in, so that you cultivate more aspects of your personality, you will automatically meet people who find you interesting. The more involved you are in the activity, the less self-conscious you will be about meeting other people. Lady Bird Johnson, the former First Lady, once said, "The way you overcome shyness is to become so wrapped up in something that you forget to be afraid."

Where the Boys Are

Many men spend their free time engaged in sports activities, either as a spectator or as a participant. Any woman so inclined has a terrific potential for meeting lots of interesting men. And that's just the beginning of the not-so-secret male hang-out atlas.

"Sailing, Sailing Over the Bounding Main"

Go to the marina on any Sunday if you want to know what many men do in their spare time. Courses in celestial navigation, and in fact any class for sailors, would be a good bet for meeting men. Sign up for a sailing class. Probably you will be put in a group with four or five other people and meet together for four to six weeks. You will have a good opportunity to make some new friends. If you already know how to sail, check out sailing newspapers for ads of men looking for crew members, or place your own ad.

Bicycling

On any given Sunday, you can see hordes of cyclists going on day trips. The ratio is usually ten men to maybe two women. There are bicycling trips for the fall leaves in Vermont, through the California wine country, and in the South of France. If you go to a local mountaineering store, you ought to be able to find a magazine advertising outdoor trips.

Golf

Have you ever tried to make a doctor's appointment on a Wednesday morning? Were you told that the doctor is not in on Wednesdays? Where do you think doctors go? Many, true to stereotype, go to the golf course. Try playing golf in the middle of the week, or just go out to the putting green and practice hitting a few balls. Or go to a driving range and practice hitting a whole bucket of balls. If you see an attractive man, admire his swing. If he has any interest in you, he'll come over to help you out with your grip.

Sports Outings

You can go on weekend outings to sail, scuba dive, play golf or tennis, water ski, snow ski, or river raft. Check into which local groups sponsor excursions. Enroll in a course or go on a trip. These are the kinds of events where you are likely to meet interesting men and women.

Conferences and Conventions

Conferences are prime occasions for meeting new people, as most people attend them with the intention of networking and making new business connections. So why not combine business with pleasure? Educational conferences and seminars on marriage and family issues are likely places to meet women, while conferences dealing with business, computers, electronics, or current events are more likely places to meet men.

Swap Meets

Most cities have swap meets that specialize in computers or electronic machines. If you're in the market for meeting a man, it might be a good time to upgrade your computer equipment. What better place to do both than a computer swap meet? Of course, you'll need help installing and learning to operate your system. Again, the men who attend these events far outnumber the women.

Compact Disk Stores

Men tend to frequent stores that sell compact disks, and sometimes you can sit and listen to the disk before you purchase it. This gives you a good opportunity to converse with others in the store. Just start by soliciting an opinion over a disk or group, new or old.

Political Events

If you have interests in the political arena, there's nothing like working on a campaign to meet men and women with similar values. Not only do you have something important in common, but you will spend many hours together and have ample opportunity to move beyond casual conversation. Even if you're not interested in working during the campaign, don't be shy about attending the victory parties on election nights. They feature free food, refreshments, and many interesting people.

Public Television and Radio Stations

If your interests are social and you're interested in the media, volunteer to help out at your local public television or radio station. These stations always need volunteers because they are understaffed and lack funds to hire more help. They always need people to help out in their yearly fund drives, or to help with specific television or radio shows. This is a terrific place to meet new people and, again, this is an activity in which more men than women are engaged.

Tours

If you love to travel, or like meeting lots of new people, you can volunteer, or even get paid to be a tour guide. Many singles groups offer tours, and going as a group leader is a sure way to interact with everyone on the trip. Even being a tour guide at your local zoo can introduce you to a wide variety of people.

Museums

Visit a local museum on a Sunday. Museums can function as a way of meeting people in a variety of ways. Most also offer classes, tours, and other organized activities. Touring the museum can be an opportunity to strike up a conversation if you are friendly and intrigued by a certain exhibit or piece of art. If you're knowledgeable about art, volunteer to become a docent and lead tours through the museum.

Auctions

If you like antiques, computers, electronics, rugs, or art, auctions are a fun way of spending time. Of course, you need to be friendly and talk with the people around you. First, sit next to someone whom you find attractive, and then start a conversation with a small remark on some piece.

Sports Leagues for Kids

If you have an interest in meeting men with children, or have children of your own, you can take care of both needs simultaneously by becoming a coach. Many divorced fathers end up with custody of their kids on the weekend. If you like soccer, baseball, or other team sports, check out the local leagues near you.

Coed Sports

Many local YMCAs or public recreation departments sponsor coed sports such as softball, baseball, basketball, or volleyball. Join a team.

Book Discussion Groups

If you like reading, joining a discussion group such as Great Books can be an excellent way of sharing ideas and gaining new insights. It is an excellent way to meet new men or women in your community who share your interests. Check with your librarian about local groups in town, or call your local college or university for some references.

Night Classes

Taking night courses is another interesting way of meeting people. Night courses are usually offered at community colleges and university extensions. Most YMCAs and YWCAs offer night courses as do most local high schools. Courses that men frequent include languages, business and finance, current affairs, computer technology, and sciences.

Trips on a Freighter

An interesting and economical way of traveling, most freighters carry 12 to 100 or so passengers on each trip. This is an "off the beaten track" way to travel, so you're bound to come back with some new adventures and new friends.

Classes in Martial Arts

This has many additional side benefits such as getting in shape, learning self-defense, and increasing your self confidence. In addition, the class can function as a way to meet new people.

Teaching

There is nothing better for meeting people than enhanced visibility. If you have skills in public speaking or have a specialty, try to teach a class through your local junior college or adult night school program. Not only will you meet the faculty, but you will also meet many students who share your interests.

Orchestras, Choirs, and Theater Groups

If your talents are in music or in the performing arts, most local colleges have courses in these areas for non-professionals. Putting on a production or a concert creates a wonderful feeling of closeness among the participants.

Animal Shows

If you love four-footed creatures, attending animal shows can be a fun way to meet new people. It also provides you with an initial common frame of reference. Animal lovers frequently find each other kindred spirits. At least, you can tolerate each other's pets.

Walking Your Dog

Another easy way to meet people is to walk your dog at a park or other place in your city where dog lovers tend to congregate. You can comment on how cute or playful a man's dog is and ask a few questions about the animal. If the man has any interest in you, he will be flattered by the attention you are willing to give his dog. Remember the old adage, "Love me, love my dog."

Walking Your Dog with a Camera

For this variation, you need to take a camera with you on one of your outings. When you see a man who suits your fancy, ask him if he would mind taking a picture of you and your dog. Of course, you then take a picture of him, and ask for his address to send him a copy of the photograph.

Fishing

Another sport rarely practiced by women is deep-sea fishing, if you live near the coast, or fresh water fishing if you live in the interior. It is a very relaxing sport, with a lot of time between strikes to chat about each other's lives. If this suits you, it's another sport you might enjoy.

Churches and Synagogues

Most churches and synagogues make an effort to provide resources for single people to meet each other. You can join a singles group at your church, or you can simply attend worship services and meet people there.

Meeting in Non-Traditional Ways

Since there are so many singles in America, singles have become big business. If you have the courage to try, the singles industry provides a variety of non-traditional ways to meet men, and success stories to go along with every method.

Singles Events

Singles events were designed for one purpose; to help singles meet each other. These events do work. Singles do meet each other. The best events are the ones that offer something to focus on other than simply meeting people, such as dinner at a fancy restaurant you've always wanted to try, a wine tasting party, a progressive dinner, a night at a comedy club, or even a lecture by someone famous or amusing. If you go to an event focusing only on meeting a man, you may become very anxious, and anxiety is antithetical to making a good impression.

Dianne Bennett, a former journalist, operates a business in Southern California called *Dianne Bennett's Personal Introductions*. Every Wednesday night, she hostesses a party, usually at a restaurant or club in Beverly Hills or on the Westside of Los Angeles, which attracts several hundred men and women between 21 and 49.

"I treat it like a party at my own home," she said, "and I greet each person at the door and conduct a kind of a mini-interview, asking them what kind of a man or woman they are interested in. A surprising number of people are embarrassed to come right out and say what kind of person they are interested in, so I use a sense of humor to tease it out of them. I say, 'Oh, I guess maybe you like short bald men with dandruff,' and then they'll laugh and tell me the kind of man they really like. If they are looking for someone who is wealthy, they ought to tell me that, too. I march them around the room and introduce them to someone I think they would match up with. Then I watch the body language, and if I can see they are not hitting it off, I go over and rescue them and introduce them to someone else."

Bennett disapproves of dancing at singles events, because she believes that most men do not feel confident about their ability to dance. She hires someone to play gypsy violin music instead, to set a romantic mood, and encourages women to dress in a romantic way.

"The men usually dress pretty well, but some women are so worried about being Respected, with a capital R, that they come in wearing some baggy blue suit. Men don't want to see women dressed that way. I say to those women, 'Where's your mini-skirt?'"

It's not necessary to dress in an overly sexy fashion, Dianne says, but she does advise women to look feminine, in silks, or cashmere, or other soft, sensuous fabrics.

"You have to turn a man on. I'm sorry, but it's true," she said. "At my parties, everybody gets a piece of my mind."

Although Dianne thinks that it is easier to meet a man at a singles event where there is no dancing, Polly, 48, has dated several men after meeting them at singles events, and she said she always prefers the ones with dancing.

"I like to dance," she said, "so I get dressed up and go to a singles event, and it has a party atmosphere. If I meet a man I like and he asks me out, that is great, but even if I don't meet anyone special that night, I still have a good time listening to the music and dancing. When I go to an event featuring cheese and crackers and conversation, and I don't meet anyone special, I tend to go home feeling like a failure instead of feeling like I have had a pleasant evening out."

At most singles events there are two kinds of people. The first kind includes attractive, bright, interesting people who show up once or twice to check out a new group or idea. Members of this group also appear when they have just broken up with someone, and want to get back in the dating scene. They generally attend one or two singles events until they connect with someone.

The second group of people are the regulars. They usually are more insecure, and they turn the singles group into their social circle. They come to the party every Saturday night, never really connecting with anyone. Obviously, the best bet is to spend your time with someone in the first group.

There is also no reason why you can't use a singles event as a good place to meet other single women. Divorced women, especially, can have few single friends, and a singles event is the perfect place to get acquainted with another woman who might enjoy going to a movie or a restaurant, or attending a singles event with you next time.

The important thing is to reframe your search. Look for ways to make new friends of both sexes, and add new activities and adventures to your life, rather than making the search for a lifemate the primary focus. People who are *desperate* to find someone are usually not very successful. They come across as too anxious, too needy. People tend to shy away from neediness. *Also, avoid the trap of attending singles events only.*

Matchmakers

Matchmaking can work, but it's utterly dependent on the skills of the matchmaker and how many potential subjects he or she can introduce to you. A Chicago matchmaking service claimed it was responsible for 190 marriages, about ten percent of its client base.

Ask the matchmaker for references. How many available men or women are in their pool? What kind of ethnic, religious, political, educational, or professional background do most of their pool have? If they don't have at least 500 to 1,000 candidates to choose from, your money might be better spent in other places.

Herschel Elkins, head of the consumer law section of the California Attorney General's office, recommends carefully checking out any company that you pay to perform a service for you. "Any legitimate company isn't going to suffer from close examination," he said, pointing out that the field of matchmaking and videodating is a virtually unregulated area, and there are unscrupulous companies as well as honest ones.

Elkins said potential customers should ask how long the company has been in business, whether it is registered with the local chamber of commerce, what is the ratio of male to female members, their ages, and where they live. He suggested inquiring if the fee structure is the same for everyone, and checking with the small claims court to see if there have been any lawsuits filed against the company.

Video Dating Services

Brenda remained single until she was 45. A high school physical education teacher, she immersed her life in her job, spending most of her leisure time in school activities. Although she had a lot of dates, she found socializing with her students more fun than her boyfriends.

At 38, Brenda decided that "My life was becoming too narrow and I decided to change. I pushed myself out of teaching. My life was unbalanced, and I wanted a permanent relationship." Brenda went back to school and became a marriage and family therapist, specializing in counseling singles.

"I thought I could help other people make the most out of single life," she says. "I really meant it."

She was approached by a video dating service which offered to give her a free six-month trial if she would recommend the service to her clients.

"That's how I met my husband. I saw him at a party sponsored by the service, and I thought he was attractive. On Monday, when I went in to look at tapes, I saw his. I requested to meet him, and found out he had seen mine and put me on his list.

"So it was a 'meant-to-be' thing," Brenda concludes. "As soon as I was ready for a serious relationship, he appeared in a catalog." A few years after meeting and dating, they were married.

Video dating services are an excellent way for young professionals who are reasonably good looking to prescreen each other and decide if they would like to meet. Meetings are only set up by mutual consent. Great Expectations of Southern California claims to be the oldest and largest video dating service, with 90,000 members nationwide.

Video dating services tend to attract busy professional men who don't have the time to attend numerous social events or go bar-hopping. Members tend to have above-average incomes, since these services are fairly expensive. Video dating services allow you to look over a man who is interested in you without having to see him in person, and allow you to avoid meeting those who don't capture your interest.

One problem with video dating services is dealing with rejection. You may select a dozen men, and find that none of them would like to meet you. If this would discourage you, then don't waste your money on expensive services. First work on your self-esteem. Improve your physical appearance so that you present a better image. You may have to screen 100 men before you find one you really like. If you are using a service and have received too many rejections, re-do your video or seek counseling to work on your self-esteem.

Advertising in the Personals

Placing a personal advertisement in a newspaper or magazine is another way to pre-screen men you might be interested in. There are two ways to do this. The first is to read the ads the men have placed, select the ones that sound interesting, and write a letter in reply. The downside to this is that the men receive many replies, and they may not answer your letter, which can be demoralizing.

The more successful method is to place your own ad. Then you sit back and wait for the mail to come with the letters from men who are interested in you. The secret is to describe yourself honestly, and to pinpoint very accurately what it is that you are looking for in a man. The more precise your ad, the better the selection of respondees you will get.

Before you write an ad, buy a magazine or newspaper and read through the ads that have been written by other women. Write down what you like about ten of the best ads. Were they zany or cute? Did they have personality? The last thing you need is a boring, non-descriptive ad.

Try to avoid these over-used words: "attractive," "young," "professional," "affectionate," "relationship-minded."

A good ad has four elements:

1. a description of yourself
2. a description of your values, personality, and living style
3. a description of how others see you
4. a description of the attributes you'd like to find in a potential spouse

Example of a successful ad:

> **CLASSY, UP-BEAT, BRIGHT AND BLACK**. Music, gourmet cooking, intimate conversations are a few of my talents. Cherished by friends and family for my openness and warmth, I'm 34, 5'6", slender. I'd like to balance my life with a man of similar values. If you're a caring, confident, successful person, unafraid of commitment and self-expression, please write to me. Photo appreciated and returned.

What makes this ad successful?

1. She describes herself with three positive attributes: classy, up-beat, and bright. She later adds openness and warmth.

2. She describes three of her talents and interests: cooking, music, and intimate conversations.

3. She physically describes herself (34, 5'6", slender, black)—but she doesn't make herself sound so beautiful that she's unattainable. Describing yourself as a 10, or as a beauty queen, may scare men off.

4. She refers to her values about family and friends ("cherished by friends and family").
5. She describes qualities she'd like in a man: "caring, confident, successful, and unafraid of commitment."

In advertising, the trick is to be catchy, witty, literate, surprising, or sincere, but however you do it, you have to stand out. If you aren't a good writer, hire someone who is. To be successful, respond to all of the replies you receive.

Another thing to consider is where to place the ad. There are national singles magazines that accept ads, but that means that the readership is located all over the United States. It is better to pick a publication with a readership in the immediate area where you live. If you have a special interest, consider a publication aimed at that audience. For example, the Sierra Club magazine accepts personals ads. If you are interested in the outdoors, or in a man who is, that might be a good place for an ad.

The Washingtonian prints an average of 400 ads a month, fairly evenly divided between ads placed by men and by women. The magazine has a circulation of 167,000, mostly within the Washington, D.C. area, and most of the ads are placed by men and women from 35 to 45, which corresponds to the readership of the magazine. The magazine keeps a tally of how many responses each ad receives. Some ads receive no response at all, while others receive as many as 100 replies, but the advertising manager believes that an average response would be about 15 replies. There have been 15-word ads that said nothing more than the gender, age, and occupation of the writer which drew 100 responses, and one-inch ads that cost $150 which received no response at all.

Alana Connolly, the advertising manager at *Boston Magazine*, said she receives a telephone call almost every month from someone who has gotten engaged or become involved in a special relationship with someone they met through a personal ad in the magazine, which runs an average of 200 ads a month. She said that a good ad attracts about 30 responses, but the range could be from five to 50.

Other city or regional magazines, such as *Philadelphia Magazine*, *New York Magazine*, *Chicago Magazine*, and *Los Angeles Magazine* all have large singles ads sections.

The magazines refuse to accept ads that are overly explicit sexually, although an ad in *The Washingtonian* that said, "Let's meet, let's cheat, let's be indiscreet," drew 300 responses.

Many magazines also have a phone-in service for replies to be left with an answering machine. *The Village Voice* ran an ad in 1989 which read, "Beautiful, long-haired blond, engaged, seeks last fling before walking down the aisle." It drew 900 replies in an hour, causing the new phone service to collapse.

An Advertising Success Story

Amy, 39, was a chiropractor with a busy private practice. She had been divorced for several years, but she didn't have much time for socializing. She felt she had used up all of the "referrals" of eligible men her friends knew, so she decided to advertise. She invested $20 in placing an ad to run for two weeks in a local Jewish newspaper. Her ad said:

> Attractive dynamic female doctor, 30s, interested in fitness, health, caring and sharing. If you are ready for the romance of your life, and you think you might be ready for me, please call.

The ad appeared on a Friday, and that night when she got home, she called her answering service to see if she had received any calls.

"Doctor, are you selling something? We've been deluged with calls for you," the operator told her.

A total of 90 men responded to her ad. Amy made a three-by-five index card for each of them, listing their names and telephone numbers, and called every single one of them back. She spent about five minutes talking to each man to find out if she was interested in meeting him. She didn't want to meet any smokers or men who wanted children, or who already had small children of their own. She didn't care what kind of work they did, as long as they seemed to be stable and secure.

"I wanted someone healthy emotionally and physically, with as little baggage as possible," she said.

Because she hates to cook, she asked if the men liked to cook, and she tried to narrow the list down to men who appeared to be seriously interested in getting married if they met the right woman.

After the telephone calls, she had narrowed the list down to 22 men she considered eligible candidates. She decided to meet each of them for a drink, one per evening, in a restaurant in the building where her office was located. She explained to the maitre d' what she was doing, so he wouldn't be surprised when she appeared with a different man every night, and so if she ran into any unforeseen problems, she could summon him for help.

Out of the first 12 men on her list, she met three that she felt she wanted to date.

"I didn't think I could manage to date any more than that at one time, so I called the other ten men and canceled the get-acquainted date with them," she said.

She eliminated one man, a museum curator, "because although he was delightful, he lied to me about his age. He was 51, and he told me he was only 48. I wouldn't have minded that age difference so much, but I didn't like the fact that he lied to try to make himself more appealing.   That said something about his need to please that I found emotionally unhealthy."

The second man, a hospital administrator, "was a nice man, but he was still raw from his divorce," Amy said, so after a few dates, she stopped seeing him.

"The third man was an attorney with two grown children.   We met in October, consummated our relationship on Christmas Eve, and moved in together on April 1.   We were married two years later," Amy related.

"He is a very mature, very wonderful man.   He had been a single parent, with custody of his children, and now he looks after me, and I love that.   I feel that I am very special in his life."

Amy was successful for several reasons.   She knew what she wanted, and she was single-minded about it. Her ad was provocative, with a hint of sexual innuendo.   (But be careful—not all the men out there are nice!) She followed up on all the responses she received and she narrowed them down according to a sensible set of criteria.   She decided whether a man was appropriate for her, sight unseen, so that all that was left was determining if they had that "chemistry" that most women look for to start with.

These are the rules:

1. Write an ad that describes you in a positive, honest way.
2. Talk to everyone who responds.
3. The first time you meet the men, meet in a public place.
4. Don't give anyone your home number until you feel sure the person is psychologically sound.

Trust your gut instincts.   Don't dismiss a man just because he doesn't pass the chemistry litmus test.   Your sex hormones don't always pick the best mate.

CHAPTER NINE

The New Dating Etiquette

$\mathcal{M}$aybe Adam and Eve had to develop their own courtship strategy, but ever since, there have always been guidelines, and often stringent rules, attempting to regulate public behavior between the sexes. Throughout history, men have been expected to make the first move. Women have had but two choices: to accept or to decline their advances. Even today, most women find it easier to make themselves available for a man to approach them, than to approach the man themselves. As recently as the 1950s, it was almost unheard of for a woman to ask a man out. The 1960 edition of *McCall's Book of Everyday Etiquette* says, "If you meet a man at a party and would like to see him again, you may not ask him for an out-and-out date, but there are ways of getting around it."

Although it is far more socially acceptable in the 1990s for a woman to telephone a man and to ask him for a date, some women are still afraid of being thought too forward. Although many men say they are delighted when a woman takes the initiative, there are some who are uncomfortable with it, so it is still an area to handle delicately.

Many successful professional women, who have no trouble picking up the check at a business luncheon, confess that they could never bring themselves to telephone a man and ask him out socially. The whole idea makes them uncomfortable. Being an accomplished woman doesn't mean that you automatically have enough self-confidence to flout deeply ingrained feelings about the roles of the sexes.

After all, no one likes to be refused (including men, who have had to risk refusals from women all of their lives), but there are techniques women can practice to catch a man's eye, to make themselves more approachable, to minimize the risk of refusal, and to take the fear out of taking the initiative.

What Makes a Woman Approachable?

Have you ever noticed how some women seem able simply to walk into a room and have men swarm around them? To the casual observer, they don't appear to be doing anything specific to attract this attention, but from the moment they arrive, men seem drawn to them. Often these women, so alluring to men, aren't even the prettiest ones.

At 41, Meredith, a college professor, was attractive, but hardly a raving beauty. Yet one evening when she walked into a singles dance and began chatting with a female acquaintance, a man who spotted her from across the room rushed up to her, dropped to his knee, grabbed hold of her hand and gushed, "Is there any chance that I am the man you have been looking for all of your life?"

Perfectly calmly, Meredith replied, "Why, I don't know. I had never considered that possibility before this very moment."

Later, she confided, "That happens to me all the time. These very aggressive men are attracted to me, when I would really rather talk to the shy ones who are hiding out in the corners."

Part of Meredith's attractiveness, undoubtedly, is the aura of self-assurance created by the fact that men always have been interested in her. She likes men and she knows that they have always liked her. She radiates a femininity and a self-confidence that draw both men and women to her.

Meredith also knows how to flirt. She's a master at the art of non-verbal communication in the courtship dance, that signals to a man, "I'm interested in you."

On another evening, Meredith was eating dinner in a restaurant with a woman friend. An attractive man at the next table struck up a conversation with the two of them, seemingly dividing his attention equally between them. Meredith was interested in the man, and she knew how to let him know. Noticing that he had a pack of cigarettes in his breast pocket, Meredith, who was also a smoker, reached into her handbag and drew out a cigarette, which she placed between her lips. The man immediately whipped out a lighter and lit the cigarette for her. From that moment on, he paid no attention to the other woman, focusing entirely on Meredith. He asked her to dance, and later asked for her telephone number.

Women like Meredith know how to be approachable, and how to take the initiative easily and subtly.

Jackie, a 38-year-old bank executive, rarely goes more than three months without a steady dating relationship. She is naturally friendly and upbeat. She wears a smile, and is quick to say "hi," and to make a passing remark or a joke. When Jackie enters a room, her carriage bespeaks assurance: she holds her head high with shoulders back; she walks with a casual but confident gait, and—a major key to her success—she's not afraid to make eye contact. Jackie looks a man straight in the eye.

If Jackie sees a man who interests her, she looks right at him and she smiles. By doing this, she signals to him that she is friendly, that she finds him interesting, and that she would like to talk to him. It's not surprising that the man she's signaling usually wends his way over to her side. When he does, she makes it easy for him by merely looking up and smiling, or by being the first to introduce herself. She comments on the gathering, on his tie, or on the food being served. The verbal content isn't what matters; she's signaled that she is friendly and wants to talk. He, feeling assured he won't be rejected, holds out his hand and introduces himself.

By contrast, women are unsuccessful in these encounters when they focus too much on their own feelings of inadequacy and their dismal memories of past failures. Arriving at a social gathering, the loser is reminded of the disappointing experience she had the last time, and so she unconsciously behaves in a manner that guarantees that the same misfortune will befall her again.

If anyone notices Maggie Morose when she enters, her shoulders slumped and her head down, they are aware that she lacks self-confidence. If a man happens to look at her, she quickly averts her eyes, so he won't think she is interested in him. She shrivels into herself and disappears to another part of the room, so he won't think she is chasing him. She doesn't look around to see if anyone is looking at her, and she certainly never smiles at anyone. She stands around awkwardly, feeling lost and out of place. She waits for a man to approach her, and if after a short time, none does, she departs abruptly—alone.

It has been another disappointing evening for Maggie, and has confirmed her convictions that she will never meet anyone and that no one is interested in her. Maggie thinks she is the one who has been rejected. The truth doesn't occur to her: she herself rejected every man in the room when she ignored them and shied away from making eye contact with them.

Maggie's chances of meeting a man are poor, because it is a rare man who will approach a woman without some kind of invitation.

Women Control the Traffic

The myth is that men make the first move. The truth is that men almost never do; it just looks that way. Studies have confirmed that men almost always need some encouragement from a woman before they approach her. Sociologist Monica Moore studied people in a singles bar in 1967 to see if she could determine any courtship patterns. She found that very few conversations between men and women were started by a man, without the woman first signaling that she was interested. Moore's findings were confirmed by a 1976 study discussed by M.S. Cary in a doctoral dissertation.

Many men will even acknowledge that they wait for a woman to give them a go-ahead before they approach her. The signal can be very subtle. A smile or repeated eye contact is the most frequently used come-on. But few men will make a move without first being given permission.

Sometimes when a woman thinks that a man has approached her out of the blue, it turns out that she actually signaled him without knowing it. Andrea, a 35-year-old journalist, walked into a party with a big smile on her face and crossed the room, nodding pleasantly to everyone she passed on her way over to greet a friend. A few minutes later, as she walked toward the bar, Calvin, 38, a surgeon, stepped directly into her path, effectively waylaying her.

"Hello," he said. "I saw you come in."

Andrea smiled and introduced herself.

After they had been dating for two or three months, Calvin teased Andrea about the evening they met, "When you set a trap for me."

"I set a trap for you?" Andrea exclaimed in amazement. "I didn't even notice you. You were the one who approached me."

"Oh, no," Calvin informed her. "You smiled at me when you walked in, and I knew you were interested in me."

Andrea's broad smile was like throwing out a net; Calvin was the fish she reeled in. She had given him the green light to talk to her, without even being aware of his existence.

How to Use Non-Verbal Cues to Attract a Man

We all like to think of ourselves as individuals, distinct from the herd, but statistically, humans are fairly similar in the way they react to certain situations. A number of studies have shown how people communicate non-verbally. Some signals are sent consciously, as when Meredith pulled out a cigarette to magnetize the man at the next table, and some are unconscious, as when Andrea smiled at everyone in the room as she arrived at the party. A man gets the message, sometimes consciously, sometimes subliminally, that you are—or are not—interested in him.

Some of the Most Common & Effective Non-verbal Cues:

Smiling

This is the easiest and most common way of saying, "I'm friendly. I'd welcome talking with you." If the man chooses to ignore this signal, there's no reason to be embarrassed about having smiled at him.

Short, Darting Glances

Look directly at the man, then look away, and bow your head slightly. Then look at him again. Repeated eye contact has proven to give men the "green light."

Fixed Gaze

Glance at a man, and then gaze at him directly for three to five seconds. Eye contact that lasts longer than one or two seconds is outside the social norms, and thus signals that you are interested in the person you are looking at. Why else would you be staring at him?

Eyebrow Flash

The exaggerated raising of both eyebrows, accompanied by smiling, shows you're asking, "Who is that good-looking man?" When visually interested, we unconsciously widen our eyes, thus raising our eyebrows. (Raising the eyebrows without a smile might be interpreted as an expression of contempt or outrage.)

Head Toss

When a woman feels someone looking at her, she unconsciously tosses her head slightly and raises her face. This is an unconsciously seductive action.

Hair Flip

It is seductive to toss your hair so that the hair swings or fluffs up, or to run your fingers through your hair, perhaps showing more of the neck (considered a vulnerable and/or erogenous area, and therefore a sign of approachability).

Lipstick Application

Applying lipstick, while either consciously or unconsciously making intermittent eye contact, is a flirtatious gesture.

Arm Flexion

Gestures exposing vulnerable areas and/or erogenous zones such as the neck or the underside of the arms, sometimes while fondling a glass, keys, or cigarettes, or running a finger along the arm or on a table, tell the man that you are ready to expose yourself to him—to one extent or another. Similarly, revealing the inner surface of the thigh, or sitting with legs slightly apart or with them crossed (hiking up the skirt) sends the same message.

Primping Behavior

A number of image-enhancing actions, such as smoothing or adjusting articles of clothing, combing hair, stroking the body, or applying lipstick, are actually ways to attract attention. These actions say, "I'm getting ready." Both men and women indulge in preening when attracted to a member of the opposite sex. A man may "shoot" his cuffs, straighten his tie, or arrange the crease in his trousers. Women employ the head toss or hair flip with raised face, or run their fingers through their hair when they feel someone looking at them.

Proximity

Another way of getting a man you are interested in to notice you is to change your proximity to him. Approach the man so that you are within "his" space. (By standards in the United States, this means closer than three feet.) Usually people turn to see who is in their space. A variation is to brush up against him, touch his arm or leg for just one or two seconds, or "accidentally" bump into him while crossing the room. This generally results in conversation.

Putting It to the Test

Ilene, 28, didn't believe that women could communicate their interest in such subtle ways and get results. She decided to test the effectiveness of non-verbal cues on an empirical basis. The next Friday night, she and three female co-workers went to a popular gathering place for singles. They walked into the bar, and Ilene perched on a stool at the edge of the group. When she saw an interesting looking man around the curve of the bar, she caught his eye, and smiled. He returned her smile, and then each of them resumed conversing with the friends with whom they had come.

Besides looking across the bar and smiling at him briefly on occasion, several times when she had his attention, Ilene ran her fingers through her hair. Once she held his gaze, and slowly stroked the outside of her forearm with one finger.

After twenty minutes, the man slowly made his way through the crowd and took the seat next to her. He introduced himself and they started talking. After a while, he made a date with Ilene for the following week.

Exercise:

Locate someone with whom you want to make contact. Use one or two of the above techniques (smiling, glancing, head toss, etc.), but don't use more; it may appear over-orchestrated or as if you're beset with nervous tics.

Everyone uses non-verbal cues, but often without realizing it. By consciously choosing small gestures with which you feel comfortable, you can encourage the approach of men you otherwise might not meet.

Speaking the Same Language

When you really feel comfortable with another person, quite often you unconsciously assume the same posture as that person. The assumption made in neuro-linguistic programming (NLP), a contemporary version of Dr. Milton Erickson's hypnotic techniques, is that one can create harmony by mirroring the posture and gestures of another because we respond favorably to someone like ourselves. More than that, by mirroring the body language and verbal language, we can get into the same mindset.

Everyone has a primary language. If you're visual, you'll see what I mean. The auditory person will hear what I'm saying and the kinesthetic person will have a feeling for my message. Tracy Cabot, in her book, *How to Make a Man Fall in Love with You*, recommends establishing a bond with a man by expressing yourself in his primary language.

This technique is employed by hypnotherapists (and successful salespeople) when they want to establish compatibility with a client. Therapists use it to help ease communication with a patient. Deliberately adopting the other person's terminology and posture puts you on the same wave length.

Exercise:

You're at a party or a singles event. You scan the room and spot a particularly interesting looking man you'd like to meet. You observe him and note that he's leaning against the mantle while surveying the group. Perhaps he's looking for someone. Maybe it's you. Instead of just marching over and blurting "Hi!", try putting yourself in his mind set by mirroring his stance. Find a wall, or doorway to lean against and, for a moment, mimic him by assuming your version of his posture and attitude. Survey the room and, while scanning the people, glance at him to see if he has noticed you. If he's looking at you, meet his eyes and smile.

Mimicking posture has other applications. If you find yourself seated, talking with a man, and he's leaning slightly forward, arms on his knees and speaking animatedly, you can lean forward slightly, hands on thighs, imitating his posture. If he's settled comfortably into a sofa, his elbow and arm along the top edge, take a similar position to convey to him that you're in a similar mindset.

The psychology behind this is that when a man feels you are like him, he feels at ease and understood. We all tend to respond positively toward people like ourselves. If you appear to be in the same frame of mind as the man of your attentions, the subliminal message is that you approve of his attitude. The "energy" feels right. This the stuff of that mysterious "chemistry"... and it is something you can help create.

You might also want to examine your own approach when scanning a room. Isn't it true you often find you're looking for qualities in a man that remind you of yourself? If you're always in the middle of a crowd, don't you seek out the man who also is the center of attention? If you tend to be more introverted and prefer being by yourself, do you find yourself looking for the men who are off by themselves?

When a couple is interested in each other, they have a tendency to lean in toward each other and create a closed circle that excludes others. They may do this by creating a circle with the way they position their arms or feet. Sometimes you will see a couple talking and one or the other, or both of them will have their legs stuck out in a manner that creates a barricade against anyone intruding. You can consciously do this to create an aura of intimacy.

Strategy vs. Spontaneity

Of course, an exciting contact can occur without a prior game plan, but if you're consciously working on increasing your receptivity and approachability, you'll be better prepared when a fortuitous encounter occurs. When you have an opportunity to go to a planned event, where there's a good chance of meeting someone, such as a business meeting, a party or a singles mixer, it pays to plan ahead.

Survey the scene, analyze your options, and determine in what ways you can encourage an approach. How will you show your willingness to make contact? Make a point of mingling; this will likely put you within range of someone you otherwise might not have the opportunity of meeting. If there's a woman (or women) at "center stage," try working the fringes by making yourself available to the men who don't want to be part of the crush. If an appealing man is involved in a group discussion, join in, even if initially you feel a little shy or the subject matter is not one of your interests.

Don't waste the occasion. Once you've made the effort to attend the event, go the distance and assert yourself a bit. After you've established contact, you're ready for the next step.

Look Before You Leap—Evaluating His Cues

Before seizing the initiative, it's a good idea to use traditional, non-verbal flirting techniques, to establish that there is mutual interest. If you're getting clear go-ahead signals, then you can try some of the more non-traditional approaches.

Rhoda, a robust woman, not unattractive but not a "10," was attending a large cocktail party. There were many people she didn't know, and among them quite a number of unattached males. Spying a very attractive man by the potted ficus near the bar, Rhoda decided to "go for it" and began her move across the room toward him. Looking around holding his drink, he appeared lost in a reverie and unaware of her approach.

Rhoda came right up by his side and as he turned, slightly startled, to look at her, she asked, "Do you believe in love at first sight?" His eyes widened in surprise, a bit of his drink sloshed to the floor, and, edging his way around the plant, he practically back-peddled his way to the other side of the room. Rhoda was dejected. Here she'd gotten up the nerve to approach this man only to be rejected. Once again she felt she'd never find a man.

Rhoda is an example of a woman acting without first evaluating the man's response. Had she stopped to consider what would make him most comfortable, her opening would have been more appropriately subtle. Now all she can do is feel defeated. She wanted to think of herself as a modern woman, able to break with tradition, but being assertive doesn't mean ignoring the warning signs. Rhoda failed to determine whether the man was at all receptive.

What she should have done was either to attempt to make eye contact with him from across the room, or to move subtly into his space. When he noticed her, she could have made an off-hand comment about the party, or the weather, or something non-threatening. If he was interested in her, he could pick up the conversational ball. If he showed no interest in her, she would feel less foolish.

To avoid embarrassment at the first meeting, you need to read a man's interest signals accurately.

1. Does he make eye contact?
2. Does he move toward you?
3. Is he leaning toward you?
4. Does he attempt to touch you?
5. Is he smiling at you?
6. Does he seem interested in talking with you?
7. Does he engage in primping behavior?
8. Does he fondle objects while looking at you?
9. Is he animated?

A man who is interested in you will display some of these obvious signs. After Calvin waylaid Andrea, who had unknowingly encouraged him with a smile, he suggested they go over in the corner and sit down to talk. He leaned forward in his chair to listen to her, and was very animated in his conversation.

When Cassie saw Gordon walk into the singles dance, she thought, "Wow, that's the best-looking man I've ever seen." She watched as he asked one woman after another to dance. When he finally walked over to get a glass of punch, she made her way over and stood next to him, ladling out a cup for herself. She put herself into his proximity, glanced at him, and smiled.

Gordon picked up her cue, and asked the old cliche, "Have you been here before?" After a short conversation, he asked her to dance. A short time later, he took Cassie over and introduced her to some of his friends, clutching her elbow as he escorted her across the room. His attempt to touch her—as well as his territorial hanging onto her—was a good signal that he was interested in her.

Men also frequently display signs of physical arousal. Arousal causes biochemical changes via the release of norepinephrine from the hypothalamus. Resulting body changes include increased heart rate, increased flow of blood to the face (flushing), faster breathing, increased muscle tension, and straightening of the posture.

Take a look at the signals a man is giving you, both consciously and unconsciously. If the signals indicate that he is not interested, you can save yourself the embarrassment of him uttering the "No, thank you," you're likely to hear if you plunge ahead.

Avoid the Desperate Woman Syndrome

In our earlier story, Rhoda behaved like a desperate woman. Her analysis of the situation was incomplete and her actions hasty and ill-timed. The man to whom she was attracted had not given her any go-ahead signals; he had not even seen her approach. She interrupted his reverie with a phrase that could be interpreted to mean that a diamond engagement ring presented the next day was not beyond her expectations.

A truly beautiful and very self-confident woman may be able, upon occasion, to get away with an audacious opening, but for most women, a little prudence is not misplaced. Seizing the initiative does not mean abandoning yourself along with all rational thought to whatever action springs to mind. It means finding the most positive ways of displaying the best aspects of your nature and utilizing these methods effectively.

Stop Signs

If a man is not interested in you, the negative warning signs are usually pretty clear. The man

1. looks away repeatedly.
2. turns his head or body away.
3. refuses to sit down with you.
4. crosses his arms repeatedly.

5. seems lethargic or bored.
6. makes references to other women.
7. demonstrates incompatibility of mood, tone, and posture.

A student of non-verbal cues will rarely suffer rejections, because she can gauge a man's interest. If you're going to take the initiative, check the road signs before forging ahead.

Taking the initiative is most appropriate in situations where the man might get away from you if you don't. If you meet a man at a party, or stand next to him in the check-out line at the grocery store, it is more important to take the initiative than with a man you see on a regular basis. If you have frequent contact with the man, such as a neighbor or someone who works in the same office with you, be friendly and approachable. You can afford to wait to see if he will make a move.

From Non-Verbal to Verbal

After you have established contact through non-verbal means, eventually you're going to have to get around to talking to the man. Avoid making Rhoda's mistake by jumping in with a too-personal, too-intense opener. Conversation should follow this chain:

1. Facts
2. Opinions
3. Personal Statements
4. Feelings

For the openers, stick to the facts. Remark on the weather, on the hors d'oeuvres, or on the other people in the room. "It's starting to snow," or "The shrimp is fabulous," or "I believe that is the Chief Justice over there in the corner." These are non-threatening, non-intimate remarks which just give the other person an opening, with no commitment.

You can move on to discussing opinions, which are sentences that begin with, "I think." The next stage of intimacy is personal statements, which begin with "I like." Finally you get around to discussing feelings, which are preceded by "I feel." It is unlikely that you will get to discussing feelings on your first encounter.

On the first encounter, talk about what is happening now: the restaurant, a movie you just saw, a book you've read, who's winning the National Basketball Association playoffs.

The first date is for fact-finding, not interrogation. Ask open-ended questions that call for more than a yes or no response, and allow the man to tell you about himself, but which are not personally intrusive. You might ask, "Tell me about the town where you grew up," or "What is it like to travel so much in your job?" Steer clear of questions relating to personal income, home, and property ownership.

Next, inquire into the man's standards and values, but avoid the machine gun approach. Try to find out how he views the world, but avoid being judgmental.

Finally you are ready to exchange more personal information about your fears, concerns, hopes, dreams, and expectations. The goal is to achieve intimacy, but intimacy grows in a nurturing atmosphere and it takes time. Rushing into true confessions too quickly can derail the relationship.

So You're Going to Start Things

You're eating lunch at the trendy and crowded lunch counter near your office. On your left is a well-groomed, blond man eating a salad and reading *Forbes Magazine*. You decide to take the initiative and say to him, "This is the first time I've been here. How's the salad?"

He looks up and smiles and says, "It's quite good. They generally have good food at this place, and good service, too."

Once you've seized the initiative and a conversation has started, keep checking the signals. Don't blurt out "Do you want to talk to me?" or "Are you single?" or "Do you believe in love at first sight?"

Instead, choose a neutral subject that will give him an opening. Talk about your surroundings or something happening in current events. Then gauge his reaction before you continue. Even a very shy man may surprise you (and himself!) by giving you a non-verbal come-on, once you've made the first gesture.

You and the blond fellow exchange a few more comments and then he says, "I don't mean to be rude, but you'll have to excuse me; I need to finish this article before I get back to the office." He smiles, you smile, and he returns to his reading.

The message is clear: it's nice talking with you, but this task takes precedence at this time. For you to press on would indicate that you don't care what's important to him. For whatever reasons, you've gotten a red light.

There are a number of other signs by which to check your progress. What does his body language say? People often cover their feelings with words (especially if they're shy), but their body language never lies. If the blond man had only nodded and pulled back, that would have been a clear "I'm not interested" signal, but he didn't do that. He looked at you and smiled, turning toward you slightly, and answered your question. He gave you an initial go-ahead, but then a very clear "stop".

Levels of Initiative

Once you've established contact with someone you'd like to see again, you must decide whether or not to take the risk of asking to see him again.

If you want to make it clear that you would like to see the man again, there are four levels of initiative, each involving progressively more risk of rejection. The first stage is virtually risk-free; it merely involves indicating that you had a good time, that you find the man pleasant company. If he wants to go no further, all you've done is offer him a nice compliment.

Level One: The Throwaway Compliment

You say, "I really had a nice time today," or "This was fun," or "I have enjoyed talking to you." By merely making a pleasant remark, you have taken no risk at all, but you have given him some encouragement if he wants to pursue you.

Heidi met John at a Little League game she attended with her married sister. John began talking to Heidi during the game and afterward they went out for coffee. Heidi enjoyed the conversation, but, because of John's mild-mannered style, she wasn't sure if she was reading the feedback correctly. When they said goodbye, Heidi told John, "I really had a nice time today. It was fun meeting you."

This gave John the opportunity to express equal pleasure without the need to commit himself if he didn't feel ready. He did not ask for her number. The next time Heidi went to a Little League game, they met again and this time John not only asked for her number, but called to take her to dinner.

Heidi hadn't been sure at first that John was interested in her and so reacted in the way that made her feel the least threatened. She offered a throwaway compliment, which was unobtrusive and non-threatening to both of them.

Level Two: The Subtle Suggestion

Follow up on the "It was great talking to you," by giving him a more direct opening: "I hope we can do this again." You have still risked very little. The ball is in his court and all you have done is established yourself as a charming woman.

Melissa, an athletic real estate broker, was attending a Saturday business buffet after an all-morning meeting. She was looking forward to a quick, chatty meal with her co-workers, to be followed by an afternoon of errands. But she noticed Gary walking up to the buffet table. As she took her plate, she flashed him a quick but very warm smile, looking very briefly directly into his eyes. Then she took the tongs and began serving herself some mushrooms.

Gary was now close behind her and she was pleasantly surprised to hear, "Those mushrooms look terrific."

Thinking, "So do you!" Melissa glanced up at him and then playfully dropped a few mushrooms on his plate. He grinned and the conversation began easily with Melissa initiating by introducing herself.

It turned out they had friends in common at the gathering. They continued to talk while loading their plates, and then found an empty table where they spent the better part of an hour in effortless, casual conversation. Melissa forgot about the other business associates with whom she had planned to lunch. As they rose from the table, Melissa made a subtle suggestion. She said, "It was great talking to you. I hope we have the chance to continue it some time." Gary asked her out on the spot.

Melissa went home on cloud nine, thinking how lucky she was that Gary had singled her out. Melissa was focused on Gary's reaction and overlooked the fact that she was the one who made it possible for the conversation to begin. She had looked straight at him and smiled. She was bold enough to drop a hint—along with a few mushrooms. And she was also the first to let him know that she would like to see him again.

But what if Gary hadn't asked Melissa out? Saying you had a good time and would like to do it again is no crime. It is a compliment to the man, and everyone enjoys being complimented.

Level Three: The Vague Invitation

This involves slightly more risk. Take it a little farther and make a casual suggestion. "I had a good time. Maybe we can have coffee sometime," or "We must do lunch." If he's not interested, he can gracefully say, "Yes, maybe sometime." If he is interested, he can set a date.

Actress Susan met lawyer Brad while researching a film role at a law library. She caught his eye when she took a seat near him and continued to make eye contact during the hour and a half she pored over the cases she had selected. They ended up walking out together and Brad asked her for lunch.

By dessert, she had no doubts she wanted to see this man again. When they parted, she said, "I really had a good time today and I'd like to see you again. Maybe we can have coffee sometime next week?" Susan had met her match. Brad topped the coffee offer with an invitation for a Saturday dinner date and threw in a delightful surprise. She'd told him she was reading for a role involving a helicopter ride, and when he picked her up Saturday evening, he took her to the airport and gave her a helicopter ride to a trendy Los Angeles restaurant in a building with a heliport on top.

But what if Brad hadn't taken her lead? What if he had replied to her vague invitation by replying, "That sounds good. I'll give you a call," and then two weeks went by with no word from him. Should Susan call him? That would depend on how well she handles refusals. If she calls and he says, "I've been meaning to call but I lost your number. How about dinner on Saturday night?" then her assertiveness has been rewarded. If she calls and he is evasive, her feelings may be hurt, but she really has lost nothing.

Level Four: The Specific Invitation

This is the most assertive technique. You say, "I had a great time tonight. How about coming over for dinner next Friday?" or "This was really fun. I have tickets to the U-2 concert next Thursday. Would you like to go?"

Rose, an executive with an electronics firm, met Hal in the course of her work. They tried to get together for weeks, but every time one or the other had to cancel because of pressing job priorities. Finally they managed an early dinner and Rose found Hal to be a caring and sympathetic person. She was determined at least to do her part for the friendship. As the evening drew to a close, she gave him a peck on the cheek, smiled brightly, and said, "Hal, I enjoyed being with you so much. I have tickets for a play this Friday and I'd love for you to join me." Hal accepted at once, letting Rose know that he was flattered she felt comfortable extending an invitation to him.

But what if he had backed away and said, "Sorry, I can't make it." A man who is truly interested in a woman but who has a schedule conflict will usually say, "I can't on Friday, but about brunch on Sunday," or some other specific occasion. If you issue a specific invitation, you run the risk that he may say no. If you can't handle the refusal, don't issue the invitation.

When to Take the Initiative

When is the right time to ask a man out? It depends on your personality and how comfortable you feel about taking risks. The other important element is how well you handle "no thank you." If you feel that if a man says no to you, you will be humiliated and never try again, then taking the initiative isn't for you. You need to be able to differentiate "no" as a refusal ("no, not now") from a personal rejection ("you aren't okay as a person").

Adopt this thought as part of your expectations: "I'm going to be refused and I'm going to refuse and that is okay." A man's refusal can mean:

1. He's not ready for a relationship.
2. He's involved in a relationship.

3. He's not sure the two of you are compatible.
4. He's had a bad day at work or is in financial difficulty. (Many men will not get involved when they are having money problems: it affects their self-esteem.)

If a man turns you down, it does not necessarily have anything to do with you. It does not mean that you're a terrible person or somehow not okay. If you were in sales and you got a "no," you wouldn't go hide for three months, would you? If someone offers you a cookie, and you aren't hungry, it doesn't mean that you think the person offering it to you is a poor cook. If you can't take "no" graciously, taking the initiative isn't the approach for you.

Shelley was 34 when she ended a nine-year live-in relationship with a man who took good care of her financially but did not meet her emotional needs. During their relationship, Shelley had worked her way up to a six-figure job as a senior sales executive. As soon as she felt financially secure, she felt strong enough to leave the relationship.

A man who worked in her office was trying to fix her up with his brother-in-law and invited Shelley to a family barbecue. Shelley didn't hit it off with the brother-in-law, but she and her co-worker's brother, George, got involved in a long conversation. George was a therapist, and Shelley found herself confiding in him about the relationship she was just ending.

"I thought about him for three days solid after that night, and finally I called up and asked him for a date," Shelley said. "I just said I'd been thinking about him and couldn't get him off my mind. I asked if he wanted to go out for dinner."

George told Shelley that he never would have called her if she hadn't taken the initiative, considering her off-limits because she was just getting out of a relationship with another man. But two years later, George and Shelley were married.

George was a sensitive, 90s man who was comfortable with a woman asking him out, and the fact that she called reassured him that she was really ready to leave her former boyfriend. George did not feel that Shelley had made a breach of etiquette by calling him; he felt complimented that she cared enough about him to go after him.

The rules of etiquette need to be rewritten to conform to the realities of the 1990s; many men feel just fine about being asked out and being complimented. It gives them a chance to enjoy another aspect of dating—being appreciated.

CHAPTER TEN

How AIDS
Has Changed the Rules

$\mathcal{L}$ove hurts, as the song goes, and in the past decade, it's become impossible to escape the fact that it can even kill. There are at least seven major diseases known to be transmitted through sexual contact, and each year there are 12 million new cases of Sexually Transmitted Diseases (STDs), according to the Centers for Disease Control. Some of these are unpleasant but go away when treated. Others are incurable, and some, including Acquired Immune Deficiency Syndrome, which was unheard of before the 1980s, are fatal.

Ironically, STDs are among the easiest diseases to prevent, but unfortunately, as *Newsweek* (December 9, 1991) put it, "Love, next to the mosquito, [is] probably the greatest disseminator of deadly microbes ever devised by the cruel hand of fate. Not only does it draw people into intimate contact, it addles their brains in the process."

Unfortunately, many people don't yet grasp that the rules of sex have changed in the age of AIDS.

In the late 1960s and 1970s, during the height of the so-called Sexual Revolution, women thought that the development of the birth control pill and the intrauterine device had allowed them to take control over their own bodies by allowing them to make decisions about contraception without regard to what their male partners did about it. Although venereal diseases like syphilis and gonorrhea had been fearsome in the past, modern medicine seemed to have conquered them, so sex seemed to have no physical repercussions that couldn't be controlled.

In the beginning, AIDS didn't seem to be much of a threat to women, either. Nobody had ever heard of AIDS before 1981, when doctors first began reporting that they were seeing clusters of opportunistic infections among otherwise healthy, young gay men. The problem appeared to be limited to homosexual men, so it was dubbed Gay-Related Immune Deficiency or GRID. Although it was immediately recognized that the disease was being spread through sexual contact, the possibility that it might eventually affect women or heterosexual men to any significant degree was ignored and even dismissed. The grave threat to the homosexual community was itself downplayed and marginalized.

The Centers for Disease Control didn't list heterosexual contact as an official risk category in AIDS until 1984, and two years later, the New York State Department of Health was still not identifying vaginal sex as risky.

The Risk to Women

But women did get AIDS. By 1985, seven percent of AIDS patients were women, and by early 1989 it had increased to 11 percent. For awhile, the experts were still guessing that most of the infected women had contracted the disease by sharing intravenous needles with infected drug users, or by having sex with bisexual men.

By the early 1990s, AIDS had become one of the five leading killers of women, and it was clear that women were getting it through heterosexual contact. Some infected women reported that they had engaged in no risky behavior other than monogamous heterosexual sex, and there has been at least one case of a woman infected through artificial insemination, proving that it is possible to get AIDS through only one exposure to infected semen.

By 1989, AIDS was the leading killer of women between 25 and 34 in New York City, and it is expected to become the major killer of women everywhere in their reproductive years.

As shocking as these statistics are, doctors still don't know much about AIDS in women.

Proportionally, there is more AIDS reported among women at an earlier age than men. But it isn't clear whether women actually get AIDS younger, or whether, because statistically more women tend to see physicians during their childbearing years, the cases are discovered and reported more reliably than among the population of gay men, who may not be getting regular check-ups.

Women with AIDS are diagnosed later and hence appear sicker and liable to die more quickly than their male counterparts. But women seldom get Kaposi's sarcoma, which is common among gay men with AIDS. The signs and symptoms of HIV (Human Immunodeficiency Virus) infection in women include low grade fevers, constant yeast infections, herpes, and persistent dry cough and sore throat, according to *A Woman's Guide to AIDS* (1989).

Doctors also believe that it may be easier for a woman to get AIDS if she already has had another STD that has caused vaginal or cervical erosions. Intercourse during menstruation also seems to place women at more risk of acquiring HIV through the blood-semen transmission route.

Mild ulceration prevalent in the endometrium of some women who use IUDS, and a cervical condition found in some women who take birth control pills, may also enhance transmission of the virus.

Heterosexual transmission is thought to be more efficient from male to female than from female to male.

Worldwide, 60 percent of AIDS infections are believed to be spread by heterosexual acts. By the year 2000 this proportion is expected to increase to 80 percent. The AIDS epidemic is firmly entrenched in the female population and projections are that it is going to get worse among women all over the world. Already, more people have died of AIDS than were killed in the Korean War and Vietnam War combined. And in the next two years, more people will die of AIDS than in the last ten years.

Yet despite an enormous amount of media attention to the problem, and the widespread dissemination of information about using condoms to prevent the spread of AIDS, many men and women continue to keep their heads in the sand.

The Most At-Risk Are the Least Cautious

When sociologists Janice Baldwin and John Baldwin of the University of California, Santa Barbara, made a large-scale study of California college students, they found that less than 20 percent of the sexually active women and men reported using condoms 75 percent of the time. They were well enough educated to know about AIDS and to know that they ought to be protecting themselves, but they weren't. In fact, the Baldwins found, "The people most at risk are taking the least precautions."

There are drugs that delay the onset of AIDS in HIV positive people, and there is every hope that this disease will eventually be conquered. Already, drug regimens of AZT, aerosolized Pentamidine, and Bactrim are controlling the pneumonia that earlier claimed the lives of many AIDS victims.

However, people who survive longer and feel healthier may remain sexually active and may contribute to a mushrooming of cases in the next ten to 20 years.

It was not until 1987 that the surgeon general of the United States, then C. Everett Koop, issued the first official national warning about AIDS, recommending the use of condoms by all sexually active adults with more than one partner. Futurists say that it takes 30 years for a new idea to really take hold. Fifteen years after a new idea is introduced, a small group of people espouse it, but it takes 30 years before it catches on with the masses. It was in 1948 that the surgeon general announced that there was a link between smoking and lung cancer, and it was not until the late 1970s that large numbers of people actually quit smoking. When the idea of non-smoking really took hold, people who had been long-time smokers felt a social pressure to give it up, because they didn't want to become social pariahs.

Camille Paglia, in her book, *Sexual Personae*, pointed out that through the ages, people have risked everything—their reputations, their jobs, the scorn of their families, ouster from their religions, disinheritance, and death by stoning—for love. She asked if anyone really expects that such a primal force can be reined in by the threat of something like genital warts? Slogans written in brochures and subway posters are not likely to dissuade large numbers of people from unprotected sex.

Perhaps not, and if it takes 30 years for widespread acceptance of the notion that women must protect themselves against AIDS, and incidentally, all other STDS, by using a barrier contraceptive such as the condom or the female condom, a lot of people are going to die.

Women need to be educated about preventing HIV. They need to know that traditional non-barrier means of contraception are no protection against HIV. They need to discuss prior sexual and drug use with their partners—but they need to know that talk alone is not enough. A 1988 study showed that women are more uncomfortable asking about sex and condom use than about drug use. And other studies show that both men and women are less than truthful when faced with uncomfortable questions about their sexual histories.

Both Men and Women Lie About Sexual Issues

A study of Southern California college students found that nearly half the men and 40 percent of the women admitted they would lie about how many sex partners they had had. One man in five said he would lie about having been tested for the AIDS virus. *Newsweek* concluded, "A partner telling you he hasn't done anything doesn't tell you anything."

Duplicity between lovers is less a problem than embarrassment about bringing up the issue. Some women worry that if they insist a man wear a condom, he will be insulted, or he will assume that the woman herself must have a venereal disease.

It is foolish to have unprotected sex. There is no reliable way of knowing what someone's sexual history is on a first date. The best advice is never to sleep with anyone on a first date. If you are going to anyway, use a condom.

AIDS Transmission Factors

Although there is constantly new research about AIDS, at the time of printing, the most up-to-date advice from the AIDS Project Los Angeles was that HIV is found in blood, semen, vaginal secretions, and breast milk. Although traces of HIV have been reported in tears, saliva, and sweat, there have been no documented cases of transmission through any of those means.

HIV and AIDS appear to be transmitted only in these ways:

1. Sexually, through direct, probably repeated, intimate sexual contact with an infected person or persons, who may or may not be showing any symptoms at the time.

2. Through the injection of blood or blood products from an infected person to an uninfected person through sharing unsterile hypodermic needles.

3. From mother to child during pregnancy, delivery, or after the child is born by breast feeding.

It is believed that AIDS cannot be contracted by:

- casual contact such as hugging, kissing, or touching
- touching objects handled by persons with AIDS or HIV
- working together in the same office
- spending time in the same house or room with an infected person
- riding together in a car, bus, or plane
- being near a person with HIV or AIDS in a public place
- eating in a restaurant with infected persons
- being bitten by mosquitoes or other insects
- swimming in public pools or jacuzzis

Safe vs. Questionable Sex

In 1983, the American Association of Physicians for Human Rights issued a set of guidelines for safe sex to help prevent the spread of AIDS. According to Dr. Neil R. Schram, chairman of the AIDS Task Force of the ASPHR, the original guidelines haven't changed much, but new data, particularly about oral sex, require some redefinition.

At the time the original guidelines were issued, researchers weren't sure whether AIDS was caused by a virus, and they didn't know which body fluids were most likely to transmit it. Because of the immediate crisis, the safest thing to do was to recommend only behaviors that didn't transmit any body fluids that might be infected. As researchers have found out more about AIDS, the guidelines have been eased in some cases and made more restrictive in others.

Some people believe that because of the severity of the HIV disease, no risk of exposure is acceptable. Some of these individuals have chosen celibacy to avoid risk. However, some will engage in sexual behavior that may not be guaranteed safe, but where the likelihood of being infected is about the same as the risk of being struck by lightning.

It is believed that safe activities include hugging, massaging, and dry kissing. Mutual masturbation should pose no threat for people with no skin rashes in places that might be exposed to their partner's secretions. If you have a rash or broken skin, particularly on the hands, you should exercise caution or discuss it with a physician.

The place to draw the line between clearly safe behavior and questionable behavior—or sex with some risk—is French kissing, or "wet" kissing. Dr. Schram says, "Since saliva is a poor transmitter of HIV, wet kissing is safe enough for most people to feel comfortable. But because there is potential for contact with the virus, wet kissing cannot be guaranteed to be 100 percent safe. If there is a risk, it is on the magnitude of one in 100,000 or one in a million."

Oral sex is another area of some concern. Oral sex with ejaculation can result in HIV transmission. Dr. Schram says that there is no proof that there needs to be a cut in the mouth in order for infection to occur. HIV can be transmitted in the vagina, the male urethra, and the anus, even in the absence of visible cuts in these membranes, he says.

During oral sex performed on a woman, partners may come into contact with cervical secretions or even blood. To decrease the risk of HIV transmission during oral sex performed on a woman, partners should use a dental dam, which is a thin layer of latex, or the female condom, as a barrier.

There is no way to make anal or vaginal intercourse 100 percent safe, but consistent correct use of a latex condom and a spermicide containing nonoxynol-9 minimizes the risk of transmission. Without a condom, there is a risk to both partners. The insertive partner is at risk because bleeding can occur in the vagina or anus; HIV has been transmitted to insertive males during vaginal and anal intercourse, Dr. Schram said.

Guidelines for Safer Sex

1. Abstinence is the only foolproof way to be safe.

2. A latex condom should be used during vaginal, anal, or oral sex and never reused. If you use a lubricant, it must be water-based. Oil-based lubricants such as Vaseline make the condom vulnerable to breakage.

3. A man receiving oral sex should wear a condom. If the woman is the recipient, she should use a dental dam or the female condom.

4. Use a spermicide containing nonoxynol-9 with the condom. Spermicides usually kill sexually transmittable germs when the condom leaks or tears.

5. Be monogamous. Mutual monogamy is preferable to multiple partners, but you are still having sex with everyone your partner ever slept with. If you intend to have unprotected sex, both partners should be tested for HIV and other STDs, then retested six months later, before proceeding.

6. Avoid anal sex. Because the blood vessels lining the rectum and anus are easily ruptured, anal sex is the riskiest form of intercourse, giving the HIV a direct pathway to the bloodstream.

Taking the Test

Although health officials recommend that anyone who has multiple partners or who engages in high risk sexual activity be tested for HIV, there is not much point in being tested unless you plan to change your lifestyle accordingly.

If you and your partner plan to be monogamous, you should each take an AIDS test, and then continue using a condom every time you have sex for six months. Then you should each take a second test. If you have had a negative test both times, it should be safe to begin unprotected sex as long as neither of you has another sex partner, according to the AIDS Hotline.

If you plan to have more than one sex partner, or if you think that your partner will have another partner, then you would never be ably to rely on the results of the blood test until you had taken it twice, six months apart, after you had ceased to have relations with anyone else.

Since the antibodies appear in your bloodstream within 60 days after exposure, there is little point in rushing out to be tested immediately after you have engaged in what you fear to be high risk sexual encounter. Wait until two months later, and then go for the test, then be tested again six months after that.

Eroticizing Safe Sex

Some women say they are afraid that the men in their lives will resist the use of a condom because they think that it cuts down on sensation or inhibits spontaneity. One solution is to eroticize condom use by making it part of the sexual ritual. It can be exciting to watch a man pull a condom on over his erect penis, and it can be a turn-on for him if you put it on him.

A wide variety of condoms are available, some with ribbing to enhance sensation, and others in colors and in flavors, such as chocolate and peppermint. Look around.

Sexually Transmitted Diseases

Syphilis

The Spanish explorers contracted syphilis when they discovered America, and the disease ran rampant until the development of penicillin. Between World War II and the middle 1980s, syphilis was under control. It is still rare, compared to other STDS, but cases have doubled since 1984. There are 130,000 cases reported each year.

Syphilis causes genital lesions known as chancres within six weeks of infection. The sores heal by themselves, but untreated, the disease advances. Within 12 weeks, most sufferers have fevers, aches, rashes, hair loss, and mouth sores. At later stages, syphilis invades the heart, eyes, and brain. The greater risk is that an infected woman can unknowingly pass the disease on to an unborn child. Antibiotics can stop the disease at any stage, but can't undo its damage.

Syphilis testing is a good idea for any sexually active person who develops genital sores or who learns that a partner was infected. Blood tests can detect antibodies to the bacterium, but antibodies may not show up for six weeks after exposure.

Gonorrhea

Gonorrhea is ten times more common than syphilis, with 1.4 million cases a year. Like syphilis, it is easily treated with antibiotics. The gonococcus bacterium thrives in moist, warm cavities, such as the mouth and throat as well as the rectum, cervix, and urinary tract. Genital symptoms include burning, itching, and a discharge. Symptoms usually appear two to ten days after exposure. If a woman does not notice the symptoms, the infection can spread into the fallopian tubes, leading to infertility and tubal pregnancy. Doctors can readily detect gonorrhea by inspecting the discharge from the vagina or penis under a microscope. Testing is recommended for anyone with symptoms or who engages in unprotected sex with more than one partner.

Chlamydia

Health officials say that chlamydia is the most common sexually transmitted disease in America. There are four million cases each year. The most common symptom is an inflammation of the urethra that causes painful urination or a discharge of pus or mucus. Like gonorrhea, chlamydia can lead to sterility in women if untreated. One in four infected men and at least half of all infected women experience no initial symptoms. Experts recommend that anyone with more than one sex partner be tested annually. Doctors should be able to analyze vaginal secretions during the course of a 30-minute office visit. Tetracycline is the usual treatment for chlamydia.

Genital Herpes

Herpes can be treated, but it can't be cured. Once infected with a herpes simplex virus, you have it for life. Some 30 million Americans are affected. Most never suffer any consequences. About 500,000 new cases of active genital herpes surface each year.

In adults, the condition is more of an annoyance than a health threat. The virus causes coldsore-like lesions in the genital area. Normally they appear within ten days of infection and heal within three weeks. But many carriers experience occasional flare-ups, and anyone with an active lesion can pass the disease onto a sex partner, even if the lesion is unnoticeable. Though herpes is not curable, daily doses of Acyclovir, an antiviral drug, can help control it.

Genital Warts

Genital warts are caused by the human papilloma virus. Nobody knows how many people carry this virus. Nor is it clear whether symptom-free carriers can spread it. But about one million Americans develop active warts each year, and two-thirds of their sex partners contract the infection. Hard, fleshy bumps appear within three months of exposure and can show up inside the vagina or cervix. Genital warts are more unpleasant than dangerous and can be removed by freezing, burning, chemical solutions, or surgery, but experts worry about links between warts and cancer of the penis, vulva, and cervix. A pap smear is the best way to detect the presence of this virus. Get one each year.

Hepatitis B

Hepatitis B affects 300,000 Americans each year, causing 5,000 deaths. Sex is the leading mode of transmission. Heterosexual transmission soared 39 percent during the late 1980s. Hepatitis B virus attacks the liver, causing a tenacious flu-like illness marked by jaundice. There is no cure. Most people recover naturally and develop an immunity to future infection. but it can take root and lead to cirrhosis or liver cancer. There is a hepatitis B vaccine which the government recommends for sexually active gay men and heterosexuals with more than one sex partner.

How to Talk About AIDS With a Partner

This is a difficult time to be single because of the threat of AIDS and other STDs. Suspicion and distrust run rampant, by necessity. In dating, there always existed the danger that some man or woman would misuse you or take advantage of you. Now that person could give you a fatal disease in the process. People who used to have misgivings about relationships are now petrified of them. And some will avoid them entirely. Abstinence and withdrawal from relationships is a valid option, but it is too bad that it is fear and in some cases unwarranted fear that drives people to make that decision.

You can't talk about AIDS without talking about sex, and in talking about sex you break a cultural taboo. People rarely discuss verbally that they want to have sex. Rather, it is all done by innuendo and non-verbal suggestion, which is partly why the discussion of contraception and protection rarely happens.

To talk about it first is to admit that it is going to happen—and usually there is so much insecurity about one's sexual desirability that to talk about it seems anti-erotic. So the conversation is frequently avoided.

Discussing sex and intimacy generates a lot of fear, even with the issue of AIDS set aside. There is the fear of being rejected, of not being valued, of not being loved, or of being left alone.

You have to discuss protection and sex *now*, before you engage in sex, if you want to be safer, feel more secure, and not feel totally inhibited in your sexual actions.

For some, the issue is fear of intimacy, but for others the fear is not only fear of intimacy but fear of sex. It's no longer just a matter of being frightened about touching someone on a deep personal level; now it's combined with the fear that you can get a deadly disease from one night's indulgence. There are those who will use the current AIDS crisis to increase their distrust: "How do I know he's telling the truth..." or "Can I trust him or her?"

Fear has always been a fundamental issue in most relationship conflicts. Fear of the unknown is always scarier, darker, bigger, and more dangerous than what is known. When relationships are just starting out, people are more vulnerable and more fearful. Talking about safe sex can be an anxiety reducer and a means to establish trust, particularly if your partner is sensitive to your needs and fears.

Asking a man to tell you about his sexual history is not a very effective way to protect yourself. It may relieve your anxiety, but it is not very reliable.

A man is not a reliably safe sexual partner unless he has been in a monogamous relationship for the past seven years with a partner who has also been monogamous. But even if he tells you this, it is not necessarily so. He may have been unfaithful, and feel embarrassed to admit it to you, or his partner may have been unfaithful to him, and he may not even know it.

The best advice is to proceed as though your partner is contagious until proven otherwise. The safest course is to protect yourself. AIDS is not a disease you can intuit in the other person. It is a disease with which you can be asymptomatic for seven years or more. It can come as a tremendous shock to both you and your partner. People have the fantasy that because they have known someone for a long time, at work, for example, that the person will be a safe sax partner. This isn't a good assumption.

How to tell your partner what you are comfortable with has always been an issue with sex and intimacy.

1. Before you have the conversation, make sure that you are knowledgeable about AIDS and other STDs.
2. Rehearse your talk with a friend. Be clear, concise and calm.
3. Discuss AIDS and use of a condom before you begin a sexual relationship with a prospective partner.
4. Choose the time and the place. In the throes of passion is not the right time to suddenly announce that you believe in safe sex only, or as one woman did, toss a condom at the man. Don't wait to bring up the subject during a romantic moment, or during a romantic meal. You might discuss it during the daytime, outdoors, during a long walk, on the telephone, or after dinner, before the touching and kissing begin.
5. To discuss AIDS with a prospective partner, you might say, "I have been feeling very anxious about AIDS and about the need to protect myself."
6. If your prospective partner seems unconcerned, you might just need to walk away. A man who has not thought about the problems involved with AIDS or who does not believe there is a need to take precautions, is probably not a good man to be involved with. You need to assess what is right for you. Would you feel understood by someone who doesn't want to be protective of you?

Although discussing your sexual history and that of your partner can be uncomfortable and scary, your discussion can also lay the foundation for a meaningful relationship, can help create a relaxed atmosphere for you to enjoy sex, and can help you protect yourself from AIDS and other sexually transmitted diseases. It is better to endure some embarrassment in discussing the subject than to risk contracting the AIDS virus.

What to Ask Your Partner

1. Have you been tested for HIV or STD?
2. How many sex partners have you had?
3. Have you ever been with a prostitute?
4. Have you ever had sex with another man?
5. Have you or your sex partners ever injected drugs?
6. Have you ever had a transfusion of blood or blood products— particularly prior to 1985 when blood wasn't screened for HIV?

CHAPTER ELEVEN

Winning by Redefining

"*A* lot of my friends have just given up," said Carrie, a 36-year-old deputy district attorney. "The men they've met were so controlling or so unwilling to make a commitment, that they've concluded that it's easier to stay home and be alone."

That's a defeatist attitude. The difference between winners and losers is that losers let life happen to them, and winners plan strategies for successful encounters. Losers wait at home for Prince Charming to ride up on a silver steed, or for their friends to introduce them to him, all the while whining and complaining about how there aren't any good men. Winners see that there are plenty of attractive, intelligent, hard-working, eligible men out there, but they know that they have to get out among them, where they can be seen. Winners give a guy a little encouragement by being approachable, having a friendly smile on their face, and being willing to make the first move by saying, "Hello," or "How's the quiche?" Winners broaden their horizons by taking part in activities that interest them and thinking in terms of enlarging their circle of friends rather than just meeting men.

Winning attitudes include taking more risks; increasing your circle in ways described in this book; reframing your goals to look for someone to be a life partner instead of someone to fulfill a completion fantasy; and being willing to utilize non-traditional means of searching, such as joining a video dating service, placing a personal advertisement, or going to a matchmaker. Winners change their love templates and redefine Mr. Right according to their grown-up needs instead of their childhood fantasies.

Overcoming Love Templates

Winners don't choose a man based on chemistry, romantic fantasies, and unconscious needs from the past. When you choose your mates according to "love templates"—an amalgamation of chemistry, associations, and unconscious psychological needs, overlaid with your own projection of the unconscious part of ourselves— you usually wind up unhappy with the results. If your mother was a rescuer and your father an alcoholic, your tendency may be to choose a man who is also a substance abuser, because playing the role of the rescuer feels familiar to you. That's choosing by a love template.

New York psychotherapist Harville Hendrix, in his book, *Keeping the Love You Find*, writes, "Out in the world, a part of us continually scans the environment for a mate.... We examine each new prospect for a fit, almost instantaneously computing how they stack up to our composite picture. Waves of incoming information are matched against the image.   Each byte registers as a 'hit' or a 'miss'— either it finds a proper receptor site, or it is discarded. Our scanner operates like a rule in/rule out screen: lopsided smile = yes; fur-rowed brow = yes; downcast eyes = no; running shoes = no; cigarette = yes; beer = no; slight nervousness = yes; narrow tie = yes."

Choosing by love templates usually lands you in a 1950s style complementary relationship. What makes a healthy relationship, on the other hand, is a balance between being complementary or opposite in some ways, while being symmetrical or similar in other ways.

The Course of Love

When you meet someone who scores high enough on your internal checklist, and magically you score high enough on their internal checklist too, you "fall in love." This usually follows a familiar pattern:

1. Recognition

The immediate sense of familiarity stems from choosing someone who reminds you of your unconscious image of what you were looking for.

2. Timelessness

Because you have projected an image of the ideal lover onto the new object of your affections, it feels like you have known him forever, because you have melded your own past with the present.

3. Reunification

The lovers feel a complementarity—a sense that two halves have become whole. Most of the couples we talked to expressed a feeling that they had "come home" to one another.

When Romance Dies

The euphoric feeling of "falling in love" is a temporary phenomenon, because it is based on the projection of your unconscious desires for a partner rather than the real person. Sometimes the bubble bursts right away, but it can last for several years. "Romantic love is supposed to end. It is nature's glue, which brings two incompatible people together for the purpose of mutual growth and enables them to survive the disillusionment that they did not marry perfect people," Harville Hendrix says.

Or as Dianne Bennett, who runs an introduction service in Los Angeles, puts it, "There needs to be a strong appeal, a basic animal magnetism, to get two people past the blah-blahs of life. Every couple has fights, but they can be resolved if you are basically passionate about each other to start with. You need that pull to get you through the day-to-day stuff in normal living."

Moving Towards Balance, Integration & Partnership

The romantic stage is followed by a testing period, when two people work out the issues in their relationship. In a mature relationship, both partners can be themselves, two wholes in a twosome, rather than two halves of a whole. In a mature, symmetrical relationship, every twosome is different, with each couple working out a relationship that is the best fit for the two of them. Staying stuck in any stage, whether it is the romantic stage or the conflictual phase, arrests the process of growth which a healthy relationship nurtures.

With pre-identity relationships, you first project an unrealistic idealization onto your partners. When that collapses, youwe polarize and reevaluate. Finally, you integrate the positive and negative in yourself and in your mate. In relationships which are formed out of individual identities (the post-identity relationship), the resulting partnership fosters the individuality of both partners, and is the expression of mature love.

The 1950s Marriage and the 1990s Model

The 1950s style complementary marriage was an economic model—based on the premise of trading services. The man provided shelter and material goods and the woman provided sex and nurturing. There was an unwritten balance sheet, a need to earn the other's contribution. In a more symmetrical relationship, love has fewer strings. Instead of saying, "I will have sex with you if you will marry me," or "I will cook for you if you support me," couples who have made the transition to a new relationship think, "I will do things for you because I want to, and because I want to be with you."

Your partner cannot be you. Your partner is a separate person. In a strong relationship, the separateness and the differences are valued. Partners are separate and equal.

In a 1990s relationship, both partners are willing to develop the unconscious side of their own personalities and to encourage the development of their partner's unconscious side. This may mean that the man makes an effort to develop his emotional side, while the woman exercises her masculine side through her career. They share the responsibility of bringing in income as well as household chores and child-care according to their schedules, their talents, and their inclinations, rather than as part of a social contract based on gender.

The Fiction of the Independent Man

"Don't let the boys see how smart you are," was the advice that Sheila, the smartest girl in her class, was given by her junior high school teacher back in 1963. The collective belief then was that the male ego was very fragile, and a wise woman never beat a man at sports or let him know that she was smarter than he was. Women were especially cautioned to be careful about deflating the "male ego" around sexuality. Is the 1990s man still so insecure and intimidated by powerful women? Is his ego frail around his sexuality?

The irony is that most men are armored with great strength and possess a good measure of the Marlboro man and John Wayne, but they are also weak and insecure. These notions are in tune with the 1950s mentality in which the agreement between women and men was to be only half a self. One of the results of the various reform movements and social experiments of the 1960s and 1970s was that people cross-pollinated. The changes in lifestyles and the longer time spent in singlehood, whether through divorce or just delayed marriage, resulted in a whole community of single men and women who really don't fit the collective stereotypes of what men and women are supposed to look like.

As we interviewed successfully married career women, we found some new patterns emerging. Men are more self-possessed and able to express their feelings. Women are more able to have an identity separate from their relationships. The kind of new relationship that comes out of this union is characterized by negotiations on a number of issues including power distribution and financial considerations, unlike the 1950s when roles were assigned on the basis of gender. It is this characteristic of pioneering the way, negotiating as they go, that characterizes the mid-life or post-identity relationship. This process of negotiation also differentiates mature relationships from the kind of relationships which even these participants may have had previously in their pre-identity relationships.

Model Couples, Old and New

In many ways, former President Ronald Reagan and First Lady Nancy Reagan typified a perfect complementary couple. He was the hero, the knight doing important work out in the world. He had the prestigious position, the power, the authority, the glory. He was strong, he took care of things. His was the face they showed to the world. She was his helpmate, the one who stood beside him and behind him, bolstering him emotionally, taking care of his personal and emotional needs, admiring him and looking up to him. She was a symbol of femininity to many Americans.

On their fortieth anniversary in 1991, Ronald Reagan said, "Forty years ago, I entered a world of happiness. Nancy moved into my heart, filling an empty spot with her love. From the start, our marriage was an adolescent's dream of what a marriage should be. And for 40 years, it has gotten more so with each passing day."

Reagan called his wife a source of strength as he pursued his political ambitions. "With Nancy, I realized my life was complete," he said. "Some people can successfully blend career and marriage, but she didn't want to try."

The Reagans are an example of the 1950s model of complementarity, in which each partner considers him- or herself incomplete without the other. A 1990s couple is exemplified by Colorado Congresswoman Patricia Schroeder, who described her marriage to her husband, Jim, in a 1989 talk to the American Association of Marriage and Family Therapists, who honored her for her work with families.

"We've always said that our marriage is not like a game. We don't have a scoreboard that says Pat 10, Jim 7, the next day Jim 7, Pat 2. That's not how it is. It is more like a partnership. We've always had a lot of fun doing it. He was very involved with the children, from day one. Now they're older and he is incredibly close to them. His friends ask, 'How did you do that?' The answer is that you don't go introduce yourself to your kids when they are 16 and say, 'Hi, I'm your dad. You look interesting.'"

Schroeder described her husband as "Phenomenal. He has always enjoyed putting people on. He wears a vest. He looks professional. I look flaky. He looks like he should be the congressman. We both went to Harvard, but he looks like he went. When we first came to Congress, they kept trying to swear him in. The speaker kept telling him to raise his hand, and he kept saying, 'It's not me. It's her.'"

Schroeder said that women who have careers and families need to accept that they can't do everything perfectly. "What I have in my house is a little sign that says, 'I'm not Superwoman. Adjust.'"

Marrying Up, Down, and Sideways

The old notion of marrying older, richer, taller, and smarter is not necessarily what will make you happiest. In past generations, when a young girl married a man to take care of her, it made sense to choose a mate who was a little older and more mature, ready to settle down and work to provide for her and the little ones who usually came along in rapid succession when there was no reliable means of contraception. However, for a woman in the 1990s who has her own career, perhaps her own condominium, her own car payments, and her own Individual Retirement Account, choosing a mate just because he makes more money or is a few years older, rules out many other men who might be more satisfying life partners.

"I'm attracted to younger men," said Doe Gentry, 45, a flight attendant who operates a dating service for older women and younger men, "because they don't try to control a woman the way I have found that older men do. A younger man is more open and willing to listen."

Doe and a partner, Dianne Bennett, hostess monthly parties for older women and younger men in Los Angeles.

"Most people have the stereotyped idea that the men who come are all looking for a rich woman, but that isn't the case at all," Doe said. "The men are from every profession and career imaginable. Most of them had mothers who worked, and they are used to strong, independent women. We have men as young as 22 and as old as 48 among the 100 or so guests at each of our parties, and the women range from their mid-thirties to mid-forties. We have better response from men, who are completely open about their attraction to older women. Women tend to be less willing to admit that they are interested in younger men, I find. I think some women have gotten so burned they would rather stay home than go out to meet someone. I drag the women I know to my parties, and when they get there, they find that they have a good time."

Doe said she personally liked men about ten years younger than herself. "I like for them to be at least 35, so they know where they are going in their life," she said. "There are some, of course, who want to be taken care of, but not as many as among older men, who I find are more accustomed to having women take care of them."

Dating a younger man, Doe said "is not for everyone. It's for the mavericks, those who are willing to step out of the norm."

Doe's partner, Dianne, said she too was attracted to younger men, "Because I'm not looking for a boss, but for a partner. I've been in relationships with dictatorial men, and I am a blonde with big boobs, so the stereotype is that I am easily controlled. Men were always telling me how much smarter they were than I was, how lost I would be without them to take care of me.   That's ridiculous.   I own several businesses and several millions of dollars worth of real estate.   I can take care of myself.   I want a man to have fun with.   I'm not saying that I wouldn't be attracted to some men who are older—I'm not totally committed to the man's being younger.   But I just find that younger men usually are accustomed to thinking of women as their equals, and that older men are bossy and put-down freaks."

Dianne points out that "Eighty to 90 percent of singles ads placed by women say they are looking for someone with a good sense of humor.   Dad wasn't all that funny.   Dad was authoritarian and boring.   If women want men with a sense of humor, they ought to be looking for younger men."

The issue of age is most important in considering life stage issues.   The rationale for marrying a man a few years older is out-of-date, and there may in fact be more good reasons to marry a younger man.   Since men's life expectancy is seven years shorter than women's, to marry a younger man gives greater odds that you will not outlive him.   And, as Doe and Dianne pointed out, a younger man may be more willing to participate in an egalitarian relationship than an older man.   Generally, a man who is within ten years older or younger than you are will have a similar cultural frame of reference, and the two of you will be able "to speak the same language." Where the age difference is more than ten years, there may sometimes be generational culture gaps, as when you still like to listen to the Beatles and he says, "I didn't realize that Paul McCartney was in a group before Wings."

Life Stage Issues

A difference in age can present a problem when it creates a life stage conflict.   Cheryl, 48, met Jason, 36, at a singles dance.   She was a college professor and the mother of two teen-aged daughters. Jason was just finishing his surgical residency and was ready to start practicing medicine.   They were attracted to each other and shared a number of common interests and pastimes.   Jason said Cheryl's age did not bother him at all, that he had no interest in having children of his own.   He asked her to marry him and move with him to Canada, where he intended to open a practice.   Although Cheryl was strongly attracted to Jason, and enjoyed his company, she turned down his proposal. Her first husband had been an attorney, and she had worked to put him through law school, and then had scrimped and saved with him during the lean years of his early law practice.

"I've been through the stage of being with a man during the 14-hour work days that are involved with getting established in a profession, and I just don't think I can do it again," Cheryl said. "My interest in Jason is not strong enough to get me through the ten years or so I know it would take before he would have the time to spend with me that a man my own age would have, after he's already past that workaholic stage of his career."

A relationship with an older man can also entail a life stage issue when the man is close to retirement and the woman isn't ready to give up her career to travel and enjoy retirement with him. Other life stage issues can involve one partner's desire to have children when the other does not.

Marrying Shorter

While the stereotypical ideal man may be tall, dark, and handsome, that is as ridiculous a guideline in choosing a mate as it is for a man to look for Miss America. There have always been short, sexy men who married tall, beautiful women. The Anne Kelsey-Stuart Markowitz marriage on the television show, "L.A. Law," with the characters played by a real life married couple, Michael Tucker and Jill Eikenberry, is a role model for women concerned with the marrying taller motto. While sexual compatibility is an important part of any marriage, the biggest sexual organ is between your ears, and it is truly what is on the inside that makes a person attractive, no matter what the packaging is.

Marrying Laterally

The notion of marrying up sets a high achieving career woman up for frustration because the more successful she is, the smaller the pool of men who are more successful.

Arlene was 45 years old and had been divorced for nine years when she decided she wanted to remarry. She had a Ph.D. in psychology, was a full professor at a large state university, and had written two best-selling college textbooks. She earned nearly $100,000 in salary and royalties.

"I sat down and thought about what I wanted in a husband," she said, "and I realized that there was no way that I was going to be able to marry up. I got out a piece of paper, and I tried to figure out the statistics, roughly. I figured there were roughly four million people in the metropolitan area where I lived, and about half of them were men. Maybe half of those were adults. That brought me down to one million adult men. Maybe half of those were over 40. So now I had a pool of 500,000 men. Then I figured that at any given time, about 80 percent of those men must be married. So that left me with 100,000 single men.

"Now, I have an I.Q. of about 150 or so, so that means only about one percent of the population is as smart or smarter than I am. That means that 1,000 of the men are smarter than me. I earn so much money that only about one percent of all men earn more than I do, so that brings the number down to about ten suitable men in my city.

"So I figured that if there were only about ten men who were smarter than I was, older than I was, and earned more money that I did, I had better start thinking about some other criteria."

Arlene decided that she needed a man who was reasonably intelligent, but he did not actually have to be smarter than she was. She wanted him to make a respectable living, but he didn't need to earn more than she did, since she could live quite well on her own income. He didn't need to be older than she was, but he did need to be within ten years of her own age, so that they would have some shared points of reference, she thought.

The next month, Arlene attended a wedding of one of her college students, and met Marvin, 41, the bride's older brother, an attorney who was in the process of getting a divorce. They hit it off immediately, and he called the next day to ask her for a date.

In a little more than a year, they were married.

"He's not smarter than I am, and both of us know it," she says. "It caused him a little adjustment, because he is not used to ever being wrong in an argument, and sometimes I know more about a subject than he does. I wouldn't dream of arguing with him about a point of law, because that's his field, but somehow he thinks he can argue with me about psychology, and I always mow him down. But while he is not smarter than I am, he is a very intelligent man, smarter than most other people in the world, and certainly smart enough to be intellectually interesting to me."

The four-year difference in their ages has been no problem, but money has occasionally been a sore point. As an attorney, Marvin makes more money than most men, but not more than Arlene. They pool their resources, but Arlene bought the house they live in with the proceeds from the sale of the house she and her teen-aged daughter shared when she was single.

"Our pastor came to visit and I showed him around the house," Arlene says. "He said, 'Oh, Arlene, this is a beautiful house. Marvin certainly does take good care of you.'"

Arlene says, "I was stunned nearly speechless. I paid for the house myself, but everyone just assumes that the man is the provider. What do they think I do out at the university? Eat bonbons?"

However, Arlene is quick to point out that the money factor is not an issue between her and Marvin. "If he had been home, he would have immediately corrected the pastor and told him, 'Actually, Arlene owns the house. She paid for it.'"

Although Arlene gave up the notion of "marrying up" and instead "married sideways," or laterally, she and Marvin have a fairly traditional, complementary marriage.

"Because he is a lawyer, and works 15-hour days, I still have to do everything around the house, as well as my own professional work," she says, acknowledging that Marvin does take responsibility for looking after her 16-year-old daughter when Arlene has to travel. "I would like him to earn a little more money, just so I could work less and spend more time on the house."

Amy, 47, the chiropractor who placed a singles ad that 90 men responded to and one of whom she married, also feels that she made a lateral marriage, to an attorney. While they both make about the same amount of money, Amy says "I am more wedded to my business than to being a housewife, and he really does more of the household chores than I do. I told him when we met that I didn't cook, and he said that was no problem because he loved to cook. After a few years, he got tired of cooking and said he thought the wife ought to cook. I told him that wasn't part of our deal. But I was willing to compromise. So now I cook on Saturday nights."

Equal Partners

One of the ways women reconcile the notion that they have not married up is to use something in their heads to tell them that the mate they chose is still superior to them in many ways. A group of friends who got together at a twentieth high school reunion were talking about the men they had married. Most of them saw themselves as equal to their husbands. Although all had careers, only one made more money than her husband. When asked who was smarter, many of them hedged making a decision, replying, "It depends on what you mean by being smart."

"My husband thinks I'm smarter than he is, but I think we're smart in different ways," Sheila said.

Marcia, 43, who has a Ph.D. in psychology, said that her husband, Ron, 46, a writer, is smarter than she is "because he is more verbal than I am. He has that high I.Q. ability—but I'm more pragmatic than he is. He has more linguistic intelligence, but I'm better at sizing up people."

And Jessica, the attorney, said that Steve, the art dealer, "has chosen a path for his life and if he had chosen to bust his chops to go to law school, he could have done that, too. I have chosen one path and he has chosen another. He makes one-third of what I make, but his ambitions for himself are well-balanced. He is in synch with his job. He's not looking for a high lifestyle, and he seems sincerely proud of me and appreciative of what the money I earn can buy us, rather than resentful."

Laurene is a therapist marrying the owner of a chain of retail stores who earns more than she does but who is less well-educated. "I'm working on my Ph.D. and he just has a high school diploma," she said. "I realized that it wasn't that I needed a man who had degrees, but that I wanted a man who was intelligent. He's into reading four books a week, so I think I have been good for him in that way."

Joan, who out-earns her social worker husband, says, "I consider that he is more successful than I am because he is more educated. I value what he does."

Although one woman we spoke to felt she had settled, most of them felt that they had chosen men who had something to offer them emotionally that far outweighed what they might have gotten from a man who might have contributed more financially.

Singlehood as a Time to Grow

Most of the men and women we talked to expressed a recognition that the time they had spent single had given them an opportunity to grow as people and to understand what they needed in a mate. Too many women spend all their time while they are single in a frantic search for a mate who meets a laundry list of specifications, instead of growing up themselves. It is a mistake to push young people to rush into committing themselves to careers and to marriage too early, resulting a few years down the line in burned-out executives, displaced homemakers, and failed marriages. Singleness is a vital stage, a time to learn about who you are, to develop self-sufficiency, and to formulate what you really want. It is also a time to learn how to connect with people and to communicate. People who figure out how to be happy being single end up with more resources.

Lovelier Love the Second Time Around

Arthur and Jean met and fell in love in their twenties, but she was afraid of getting involved with him and sent him away. He married another woman, but two decades later, after he was divorced, he and Jean met again, and this time they made an effort to make the relationship work.

"I'd had a marriage under my belt and was twenty years further down the road in my professional and experiential life," Arthur said, "so I knew what it was to have a partner and to make competent decisions about a household."

Arthur's first wife was from a different country, whereas Jean was from his hometown. "Language is a very important part of communication. With Jean the language and interaction were very different from how it had been with my first wife. Even our senses of humor were the same," Arthur said. "Not only the words were different with my first wife, but the commonalities of thought. Jean and I both laugh at the same stupid things."

Arthur repeated the same theme as many of the other couples we interviewed: "With Jean, it was like coming home to part of myself."

Arthur remembers that when he first met Jean, "I'd been out with other girls, but I had never met anyone else like her. I actually never thought of anyone but her. I was completely absorbed in her. I had been happy with other girls before, but never so absorbed, so single-minded as I was with her."

When Jean broke off with him, "I was very hurt. The woman I later married was a good woman, but a part of me has always been with Jean. It was left with her and stayed with her and was never taken up until I met her again. The day I met her again, when I was divorced and in my mid-forties, it was exactly the same as the day I met her before. I was very single-minded about her."

Arthur continued, "My first wife was lovely woman, but there was always this thing missing. I actually had fallen for Jean, way back, and she had a depth and an experience and I'd been deprived of it. When I met her again and we could be together, that sort of blossomed. The most romantic time of my life was when we met again. We knew we were going to be together and that was a very special time."

Jean also describes her relationship with Arthur as being "Like coming home. We had a history together. It felt very much like coming home. All the things I valued in him before I still valued, and the things I didn't like before, I felt now that I could tolerate. We have a very equal relationship. In my twenties I was not as evolved. At 22 I was still in the role that I felt I needed a man to take care of me. It was not something I had been taught by my parents, but just something that the society around me had foisted onto me. This time in my life, I didn't need any one to look after me. I was perfectly able to take care of myself. This time I was looking for a relationship with someone."

Are You Ready For a Post-Identity Relationship?

You're ready for a post-identity relationship if you feel okay about yourself, no matter what he says. If you have a strong sense of your own identity, you don't need to be what a man wants you to be. It is nice, of course, for him to approve of what you are, but you need to be sure of yourself, no matter what he thinks. To a degree, everyone does things to please someone they love, but to do everything to be who someone else wants you to be is not good for you.

Some theorists believe many of the problems that affect women, such as eating disorders, anxiety, and depression, are a result of women not being able to internalize that they are okay. Many single women obsessively lament how flawed their bodies are. They only really feel good about the way they look when a man accepts them. His approval of their body is the validation they need.

If you worry "Is my body okay? Will somebody love me?" the answer is yes, if you accept yourself the way you are. If you think you're good enough, someone else will too.

Real Love

All couples realize eventually that their mate cannot fulfill all of their dreams and expectations and that their life together will fall short in some ways from what they read about in fairy tales. Couples who stay together anyway are the ones who are willing to abandon their fantasies and build a mature relationship built on valuing and honoring each other's individuality. Real love begins after the illusions wear off, when you realize that your partner is not as perfect as you thought. Characteristics that once seemed endearing have become annoying, and you see each other as real people instead of heroes and heroines. In enduring relationships, the couple stays together and they build a love based on who they really are.

In her book, *Married People, Staying Together in an Age of Divorce*, Francine Klagsbrun writes that "Marriage is a process because it is always in flux, it never stays the same and it never completes itself. It is a process of changing and accepting change, of settling differences and living with differences that will never be settled, of drawing close and pulling apart and drawing close again. The one unchanging and constant in a marriage is the attachment of the couple to one another—the commitment to use today's terminology. Yet even that is not static, but is constantly in motion. At the heart of that commitment lies an unresolvable tension, a pull between oneself and one's partner. It's a pull between loving yourself and loving your partner, doing for yourself and doing for your partner, satisfying yourself and satisfying your partner. If you don't love yourself, you cannot love another person, because how can you value the other's needs when you don't place value on your own needs? But if you love yourself too much, then how can you give love to the other?"

Couples who decide to stay together, and who find their marriage to be a nurturing and joyful union, are the ones whose attachment to each other is greater than the disillusionment when the early romance wanes. They love themselves and they love their partner, and they are willing sometimes to place the other person's needs above their own, knowing that the other person will do the same for them on another occasion. They regard the compromise not as self-sacrifice, but as self-enhancement, because in caring for their partner, they are also nurtured.

When all is said and done, couples who seem happiest are the ones who say that their mate is their best friend. After you put aside the facades, the roles you play, the conflicts, and the power struggles, couples who endure over time share a true liking for the other person. They have the same values, similar backgrounds, some similar and some opposite personality traits, a strong sexual compatibility, a willingness to accommodate differences, and skills to negotiate. But most of all, couples who stay together share a strong sense of friendship. Many of the couples we spoke to echoed the same expression—they said that with their partner, they felt that they had come home.

"He's my best friend," Sheila said. "In the final analysis, that's what keeps us together."

Bibliography

Ahrons, C.R.H. and Rodgers, R. (1987). *The Divorced Family*. New York: Norton.

AIDS Project, L.A. (1985). "Safe Sex Practices."

AIDS Project, L.A. (1992). "Letter on Current Transmission Routes."

AIDS Project of the East Bay. "Safer Sex: A Guide for Everyone Concerned About AIDS." County of Los Angeles, Public Health.

Allen, S.C. (1987). "The Relation of Income and Sex-Role Orientation in Dual Worker Marriages Where the Wife is Self-Employed and Earns the Greater Income," unpublished dissertation, University of Iowa.

Aronson, E. (1984). *The Social Animal*. New York: W.H. Freeman and Co.

Bahr, S.J. (1974). "Effects on Power and Division of Labor in the Family". Hoffman, L.W. and Nye, I. (Eds.) 1974, *Working Mothers*. San Francisco: Jossey-Bass.

Bailey, B. (1988). *From Front Porch to Back Seat: Courtship in Twentieth Century America*. Baltimore: Johns Hopkins University Press.

Balswick, J. (1988). *The Inexpressive Male*. Lexington, MA: Lexington Books.

Bandler, R. and Grindler, J. (1975). *The Structure of Magic*. Palo Alto: Science and Behavior.

Bane, M.J. (1976). "Here to Stay: Parents and Children." Skolnick, A.S., and Skolnick, J.H. (Eds.) (1989). *Rethinking Marriage, Sexuality, Child Rearing, and Family Organization*. Glenview, Ill: Scott, Foresman and Co.

Barbach, L. (1975). *For Yourself*. New York: New American Library.

Barnett, R.C. and Baruch, G.K. (1987). "Determinants of Fathers' Participation in Family Work." *Journal of Marriage and Family*, Vol 49, 29-40, Feb.

Barnett, R.C. and Baruch, G.K. (1987). "Mothers' Participation in Childcare: Patterns and Consequences." Crosby, F.J. (Ed.) (1987) *Spouse, Parent, Worker: On Gender and Multiple Roles*. New Haven: Yale University Press.

Barnett, R.C. and Baruch, G.K. (1985). "Women's Involvement in Multiple Roles and Psychological Distress." *Journal of Personality and Social Psychology*, Vol. 49:1, 135-145.

Baruch, G.K. and Barnett, R.C. (1981). "Fathers' Participation in the Care of Their Preschool Children". *Sex Roles*, Vol. 7 (10), 1043-1055.

Baruch, G.K. and Barnett, R.C., (1987). "Role Quality and Psychological Well-Being." Crosby, F.J. (Ed.) (1987). *Spouse, Parent, Worker: On Gender and Multiple Roles*, New Haven: Yale University Press.

Baruch, G.K. and Barnett, R.C. (1986). "Consequences of Fathers' Participation in Family Work: Parents' Role Strain and Well-Being." *Journal of Personality and Social Psychology*, 51:5, 983-992.

Baruch, G.K. and Barnett, R.C. (1986). "Role Quality, Multiple Role Involvement, and Psychological Well-Being in Midlife Women." *Journal of Personality and Social Psychology*, 51:3, 578-585.

Baruch, G.K. et al, (1987). "Women and Gender in Research on Work and Family Stress." *American Psychologist*, 42,2, 130-136, Feb.

Bates, M. and Keirsey, D.W., (1978). *Please Understand Me*. Del Mar, CA: Prometheus Nemesis Book Co.

Bateson, G. (1972). *Steps to an Ecology of Mind*. New York: Ballantine Books.

Beer, W.R. (1983). *Househusbands: Men and Housework in American Families*. New York: Praeger.

Belenky, M.F., Clinchy, B.M., Goldberger, N.R., and Tarule, J. (1986). *Women's Ways of Knowing*. New York: Basic Books.

Bem, S.L. (1974). "The Measurement of Psychological Androgyny." *Journal of Consulting and Clinical Psychology*, Vol. 42 (2), 155-162.

Berger, P. and Luckmann, T. (1966). *Social Construction of Reality*. New York: Doubleday & Co.

Bergman, M. (1987). *The Anatomy of Love*. New York: Columbia University Press.

Bernard, J. (1972). *Future of Marriage*. New York: World.

Bernard, J. (1975). *Women, Wives, Mothers: Values and Options*. Chicago: Aldine.

Bernard, J. (1989). "The Good-Provider Role: Its Rise and Fall." Skolnick, A.S., and Skolnick, J.H. (Eds.) (1989). *Rethinking Marriage, Sexuality, Child Rearing, and Family Organization*. Glenview, Ill: Scott, Foresman and Co.

Berne, E. (1964). *Games People Play*. New York: Grove Press.

Blood, R.O., Jr., and Wolfe, D.M. (1960). *Husbands and Wives: The Dynamics of Married Living*. Glencoe, Ill.: The Free Press.

Blumstein, P. and Schwartz, P., "American Couples," (excerpted 1983). Skolnick, A.S., and Skolnick, J.H. (Eds.) (1989). *Rethinking Marriage, Sexuality, Child Rearing, and Family Organization*. Glenview, Ill: Scott, Foresman and Co.

Bly, R. (1990). *Iron John*. Reading, MA: Addison-Wesley Publishing Co., Inc.

Bly, R. (1981). "The Masculine", talk in April to the C.G. Jung Institute, Los Angeles.

Boston Women's Collective (1973). *Our Bodies, Our Selves*. New York: Simon and Schuster.

Bowen, M. (1978). *Family Therapy in Clinical Practice*. New York: Aronson.

Branden, N. (1980). *The Psychology of Romantic Love.* Los Angeles: Jeremy P. Tarcher, Inc.

Bryant, F.B., and Veroff, J., (1982). "The Structure of Psychological Well-being: A Sociohistorical Analysis." *Journal of Personality and Social Psychology.* Vol. 43 (4) 653-673.

Bryant, F.B., and Veroff, J., (1984). "Dimensions of Subjective Mental Health in American Men and Women." *Journal of Health and Social Behavior.* Vol. 25 (2) 116-135.

Cabot, T. (1984). *How To Make a Man Fall in Love with You.* New York: Dell Publishing.

Carter, B. and McGoldrick, M. (1990). *The Changing Family Life Cycle.* Boston, MA: Allyn and Bacon.

Cary, M.S., (1976). *Talk? Do You Want to Talk?* Unpublished dissertation, University of Pennsylvania.

Cassell, C. (1984). *Swept Away.* New York: Simon and Schuster.

Cath, S., Gurwitt, A., and Gunsberg, L. (Eds), (1989). *Fathers and Their Families.* Hillsdale, N.J.: Analytic Press.

Cherlin, A.J. (1981). *Marriage, Divorce, Remarriage.* Cambridge: Harvard University Press.

Chodorow, N. (1978). *The Reproduction of Mothering.* Berkeley: University of California Press.

Clatterbaugh, K. (1990). *Contemporary Perspectives on Masculinity.* Boulder: Westview Press.

Coleman, L. M., Antonucci, T. C., and Adelmann, P.K. (1987). "Role Involvement, Gender and Well-Being." Crosby, F.J.(Ed.) (1987). *Spouse, Parent, Worker: On Gender and Multiple Roles.* New Haven: Yale University Press.

Cowan, C. P. and Cowan, P. A. (1987). "Men's Involvement in Parenthood: Identifying the Antecedents and Understanding the Barriers." Berman, P. W. and Pederson, F.A. (Eds) (1987). *Men's Transitions to Parenthood, Longitudinal Studies of Early Family Experience.* Hillsdale, N.J.: Lawrence Erlbaum Associates.

Cowan, C. and Kinder, M. (1985). *Smart Women, Foolish Choices.* New York: New American Library.

DeShazer, S. (1982). *Patterns of Brief Family Therapy,* New York: Guilford Press.

DeShazer, S. (1984). *The Death of Resistance, Family Process,* 23:1, p. 11-17.

Eisendrath-Young, P.L. and Wiedmann, F. (1987). *Female Authority.* New York: Guilford Press.

Erikson, E. (1968). *Identity Youth and Crisis.* New York: W.W. Norton.

Erikson, E., (1950). *Childhood and Society.* New York: W.W. Norton

Evans, B., McCormack, S.M., Bond, R.A., and MacRae, K.D. (1991). "Trends in Sexual Behavior and HIV Testing Among Women Presenting at a Genitourinary Medicine Clinic During the Advent of AIDS." *Genitourinary Medicine,* 1991, Jun, 67 (3): 194-8.

Faludi, S. (1991). *Backlash.* New York: Crown Publishers.

Farrell, Michael P. (1976). "Friendship Between Men." Lewis, R. A. and Sussman, M.B. (Eds.) (1986). *Men's Changing Roles in the Family*, New York: Haworth Press.

Fast, J. (1970). *Body Language*. N.Y.: Simon & Schuster.

Festinger, L. (1957). *A Theory of Cognitive Dissonance*, Stanford: Stanford University Press.

Gardner, H. (1985). *Frames of Mind: The Theory of Multiple Intelligences.* Cambridge: Harvard University Press.

Garnets, L., and Pleck, J.H. (1979). "Sex Role Identity, Androgyny, and Sex Role Transcendence: A Sex Role Strain Analysis." *Psychology of Women Quarterly*, Vol 3 (3), 270-283.

Gergen, K.J. (1985). "The Social Constructionist Movement in Modern Psychology." *American Psychologist*, Vol. 40 (3), 266-275.

Giele, J.Z. (1978). "Changing Sex Roles and Family Structure." Voydanoff, P. (Ed.). (1984). *Work and Family: Changing Roles of Men and Women*. Palo Alto: Mayfield Publishing Co.

Giler, J.Z. (1990). "Theoretical Constructions in Family Therapy: Current Trends." Unpublished paper.

Giler, J.Z. (1991). "Collusion in Couples: The Narcissistic-Borderline Dance." Unpublished paper.

Giler, J.Z. (1992). "Sex Roles and Gender." Unpublished paper.

Gilligan, C. (1982). *In a Different Voice*. Cambridge: Harvard University Press.

Gong, V. and Rudnick, N. (1986). *AIDS: Facts and Issues.* New Brunswick: Rutgers University Press.

Gottman, J.M, and Krofoff, L.J. (1989). "Marital Interaction and Satisfaction: A Longitudinal View." *Journal of Consulting and Clinical Psychology*, Vol. 57, p. 47-52.

Gove, W. R. and Zeiss, C. (1987). "Multiple Roles and Happiness." Crosby, Faye J. (Ed.) (1987). *Spouse, Parent, Worker: On Gender and Multiple Roles.* New Haven: Yale University Press.

Grant, T. (1988). *Being A Woman.* New York: Random House.

Grossman, F.K. (1987). "Separate and Together." Kimmel, M. S. (Ed) (1987). *Changing Men: New Directions in Research on Men & Masculinity.* Newbury Park: Sage.

Haas, L. (1980). "Sexual Equality in the Family: Study of Role Sharing Couples." *Family Relations*, July, Vol. 29:3.

Hall, D.T. (1972). "A Model of Coping with Conflict: The Role Behavior of College Educated Women." *Administrative Science Quarterly*, Vol. 4, p. 471-486.

Hall, F.S. and Hall, D.T. (1979). *The Two-Career Couple*. Reading, MA: Addison-Wesley.

Hare-Mustin, R.T. and Marecek, J. (1988). "The Meaning of Difference: Gender Theory, Postmodernism, and Psychology." *American Psychologist*, Vol 43 (6), p. 455-464.

Hareven, T.K. (1982). "American Families in Transition: Historical Perspectives on Change." Skolnick, A.S., and Skolnick, J.H. (Eds.) (1989). *Rethinking Marriage, Sexuality, Child Rearing, and Family Organization*. Glenview, Ill: Scott, Foresman and Co.

Hiller, D.V. and Philliber, W.W. (1986). "The Division of Labor in Contemporary Marriage: Expectations, Perceptions, and Performance." Skolnick, A.S., and Skolnick, J.H. (Eds.) (1989). *Rethinking Marriage, Sexuality, Child Rearing, and Family Organization*. Glenview, Ill: Foresman and Co.

Hite, S. (1976). *The Hite Report: A Nationwide Study of Female Sexuality*. New York: Bell Publishing.

Hite, S. (1991). *The Hite Report of Male Sexuality*. New York: Ballantine Books.

Hite, S. (1987). *Women and Love: A Cultural Revolution in Progress*. New York: Knopf.

Hoffman, L.W. and Nye, I. (1974). *Working Mothers*, San Francisco: Jossey-Bass.

Hoffman, L. (1990). "Constructing Realities: An Art of Lenses", *Family Process*, 29:1, March.

Hoffman, L., (1985). "Beyond Power and Control: Toward a 'Second Order'", *Family Systems*, vol 3 (4), p. 381-396. Winter.

Holahan, C.K., and Gilbert, L.A. (1979). "Conflict Between Major Life Roles: Women and Men in Dual Career Couples." *Human Relations*, Vol. 32 (6), 451-467.

Holmstrom, L.L. (1972). *The Two Career Family*. Cambridge: Schenkman.

Holter, H. (1975). "Sex Roles & Social Change." Mednick, M. et. al. (Ed.) (1975). *Women & Achievement*. New York: John Wiley & Sons.

Hoopes, M.M., and Harper, J.M. (1987). *Birth Order Roles & Sibling Patterns in Individual and Family Therapy*. Rockville, MD: Aspen Publications.

Horner, M. (1970). "Femininity and Successful Achievement". Walker, E. (Ed.). *Feminine Personality and Conflict*. Westport: Greenwood Press.

Horney, K. (1967). *Female Psychology*. New York: W.W. Norton.

Hornung, C.A., McCullough, B.C., and Sugimoto, T. (1981). "Status Relationships in Marriage: Risk Factors in Spouse Abuse." *Journal of Marriage and Family Therapy*. 43, 675-692.

Johnson, R. (1976). *He*. King of Prussia, PA: Religious Publishing Co.

Johnson, R. (1983). *We: Understanding the Psychology of Romantic Love*. San Francisco: Harper and Row.

Josselson, R. (1987). *Finding Herself*. San Francisco: Jossey Bass.

Jung, C.G. (1971). *Psychological Types*. Princeton, N.J.: Princeton University Press.

Kelly, G.A. (1955). *A Theory of Personality: The Psychology of Personal Constructs*. N.Y.: W.W. Norton.

Kernberg, O. (1976). "Mature Love: Prerequisites and Characteristics." Kernberg, O. (Ed.) *Object Relations Theory and Clinical Psychoanalysis*. New York: Jason Aronson.

Key, M.R. (1975). *Male/Female Language*. Metchen, N.J: Scarecrow Press.

Kimmel, M. (1987). "Teaching a Course on Men." Kimmel, M. (Ed.) (1987). *Changing Men: New Directions in Research on Men & Masculinity*. Newbury Park: Sage.

Klagsbrun, F. (1985). *Married People Staying Together in the Age of Divorce*. New York: Bantam Books.

Knapp, M.L. (1978). *Nonverbal Communication in Human Interaction*. New York: Holt, Reinhart, and Winston.

Kroeger, O. and Thuesen, J.M., (1988). *Type Talk*. New York: Dell Publishing.

LaPlatney, R. (1991). "Women and AIDS: The Evolution of an Epidemic." *Journal of the New York State Nurses Assoc.*, 1991, June, 22 (2): 18-22.

Lein, L. (1979). "Male Participation in Home Life: Impact of Social Supports and Breadwinner Responsibility on the Allocation of Tasks." Voydanoff, P.(Ed.) (1984). *Work and Family: Changing Roles of Men and Women*. Palo Alto: Mayfield Publishing Co.

Levin, L. and Bellotti, L.G. (1992). *You Can't Hurry Love*. New York: Dutton.

Levine, J.A. (1976). *Who Will Raise the Children: New Options for Fathers (and Mothers)*. Philadelphia: J.B. Lippincott Co.

Levinson, D.J., Darrow, C.N., Klein, E.B., Levinson, M.H. and McKee, B. (1978). *The Seasons of a Man's Life*. New York: Ballantine Books.

Lewis, R.A. (1986). "Men's Changing Roles in Marriage and the Family." Lewis, R.A. and Sussman, M.B. (Eds) (1986). *Men's Changing Roles in the Family*, New York: Haworth Press.

Loevinger, J. (1976). *Ego Development*. San Francisco: Jossey Bass.

Luepnitz, D. (1988). *The Family Interpreted: Feminist Theory in Clinical Practice*. New York: Basic Books.

Maccoby, E.E., and Jacklin, C.N. (1974). *The Psychology of Sex Differences*. Stanford: Stanford University Press.

Maccoby, E.E. (1988). "Gender As a Social Category." *American Psychologist*, Vol. 24 (6) 755-765.

Maccoby, E.E. (1990). "Gender and Relationships." *American Psychologist*, Vol 45 (4), 513-520.

Mahler, M. (1975). *The Psychological Birth of the Human Infant*. New York: Basic Books.

Martelli, L.J., Peltz, F.D. and Messina, W. (1987). *When Someone You Know Has AIDS*. New York: Crown Publishers.

Mayer, K.H. and Carpenter, C.C.J., (1992). "Women and AIDS," *Scientific American*, March, 1992.

McBride, A.B. (1990). "Effects of Women's Multiple Roles", *American Psychologist*, (March) Vol. 45 (3), 381-284.

McKay, M., Davis, M. and Fanning, P. (1983). *Messages, The Communication Skills Book*. Oakland, CA: New Harbinger Publications.

McLaughlin, D., Bill, J.O., Johnson, T.R., Melber, B.D., Winges, L.D. and Zimmerie, D.M. (1986). *Batelle Study: The Cosmopolitan Report on the Changing Life Course of American Women*. 3 Volumes, summary report. New York: Hearst Magazine.

Mednick, M.T., (1987). "Single Mothers: A Review and Critique of Current Research." Skolnick, A.S., and Skolnick, J.H. (Eds.) (1989). *Rethinking Marriage, Sexuality, Child Rearing, and Family Organization*. Glenview, Ill.: Scott, Foresman, and Co.

Mercer, R.T., Nichols, E.G., and Doyle, G.C. (1989). *Transitions in a Woman's Life: Major Life Events in Developmental Context*. New York: Springer Publishing Co.

Miller, M. B. (1976). *Toward a New Psychology of Women*. Boston: Beacon Press.

Moen, P., (1982). "Two Provider Family: Problems & Potentials." Lamb, M.E. (Ed.) (1982). *Nontraditional Families: Parent and Child Development*. Hillsdale, N.J.: Lawrence Erlbaum.

Moody, Jr., R.A. (1978). *Laugh after Laugh: The Healing Power of Humor*. Jacksonville, FL: Headwaters Press.

Moore, M. (1985). "Nonverbal Courtship Patterns in Women," *Ethnology and Sociobiology*, 6:237-247.

Morris, D. (1971). *Intimate Behavior*. New York: Random House.

Nelson, S. (1992). "Talking Smart, Acting Stupid about AIDS," *Glamour*, February, 1992.

Nierenberg, G.I., (1981). *The Art of Negotiating*. New York: Simon and Schuster.

Norwood, R. (1985). *Women Who Love Too Much*. Los Angeles: Jeremy P. Tarcher, Inc.

Paglia, C. (1990). *Sexual Personae: Art and Decadence from Nefertiti to Emily Dickinson*. New Haven: Yale University Press.

Parson, T. and Bales, R. (1955). *Family, Socialization and Interaction Process*, New York: Free Press.

Paul, J. and Paul, M. (1983). *Do I Have to Give Up Me to Be Loved By You?* Minneapolis, MN.: CompCare Publications.

Pedersen, F.A. (1985). "Research and the Father: Where Do We Go From Here?" Hanson, S.M.H. and Bozett, F. W. (Eds.) (1985) *Dimensions of Fatherhood*, Newbury Park: Sage.

Pleck J. and Sawyer, J. (Eds) (1974). *Men and Masculinity*, Englewood Cliffs, N.J.: Prentice-Hall.

Pleck, J.H. and Lang, L. (1978). *Men's Family Role: It's Nature and Consequences*. Wellesley, MA: Wellesley College Center for Research on Women.

Pleck, J.H. (1985). *Working Wives, Working Husbands*. Beverly Hills, CA: Sage.

Poloma, M.M. and Garland, T.N. (1973). "Role Conflict and the Married Professional Woman." Young and Willmott (Eds). (1973) *The Symmetrical Family*. New York: Pantheon.

Pye, F. (1973). "Feminine Images of Success," *Psychological Perspectives*, 4:2, Fall.

Robinson, J., Juster, T. and Stafforde, F. (1976). *American's Use of Time*, Ann Arbor, MI: Institute for Social Research.

Rosenblum, K.E. (1986). "Conflict Between and Within Genders." Skolnick, A.S., and Skolnick, J.H. (Eds.) (1989). *Rethinking Marriage, Sexuality, Child Rearing, and Family Organization*. Glenview, Ill: Scott, Foresman and Co.

Rossi, A.S. (1968). "Transition to Parenthood." Skolnick, A.S., and Skolnick, J.H. (Eds.) (1989). *Rethinking Marriage, Sexuality, Child Rearing, and Family Organization*. Glenview, Ill.: Scott, Foresman and Co.

Russell, G. (1983) *The Changing Role of Fathers*. St. Lucia, Australia: University of Queensland Press.

Safilios-Rothchild, C. (1970). "The Study of Family Power Structure: A Review", 1960-1969. *Journal of Marriage and the Family*, Vol. 32, 539-552.

Sanford, J.A. (1980). *The Invisible Partners*. New York: Paulist Press.

Sarbin, T.R. and Allen V.L. (1968). "Role Theory." G. Linzey & E. Aronson (Eds.) *The Handbook of Social Psychology*, Vol. 1, 2nd ed. pp. 488-567. Reading, MA: Addison, Wesley.

Scanzoni, J.H. (1975). *Sex Roles, Life Styles & Childbearing: Changing Patterns in Marriage and the Family*. New York: Free Press.

Scanzoni, J. H. (1978). *Sex Roles, Women's Work & Marital Conflict*. Lexington: Lexington Books.

Schram, N.R. (1990). "Refining Safer Sex," *Focus*. June, 1990.

Schroeder, P. (1989). "Awards Dinner Address," AAMFT, October, 1989. San Francisco.

Sekaran, U. (1986). *Dual Career Families*. San Francisco: Jossey-Bass.

Seligmann, J., Beachy, L., Gordon, J., McCormick, J. and Starr, M. (1991). "Safer Sex," "Sleeping with the Enemy," "Condoms in the Classroom," *Newsweek*. December 9, 1991, Vol. CXVIII, No. 24.

Sheehy, G. (1976). *Passages*. New York: E.P. Dutton.

Springer, S. P. and Deutsch, G. (1985). *Left Brain, Right Brain*. New York: W. H. Freeman & Co.

Staines, G.L. (1986). "Men's Work Schedules and Family Life." Lewis, R.A. and Sussman, M.B. (Eds.) *Men's Changing Roles in the Family*. New York: Haworth Press.

Staines, G.L., Pleck, J.H., Shepard, L. and O'Connor, D. (1978). "Wives' Employment Status and Marital Adjustment: Yet Another Look." *Psychology of Women Quarterly*. Vol. 3, 90-120.

Steil, J.M. and Turetsky, B.A. (1987). "Marital Influence Levels and Symptomatology Among Wives." Crosby, F. J. (Ed.) *Spouse, Parent, Worker: On Gender and Multiple Roles*. New Haven: Yale University Press.

Steiner, C. (1971). *Games Alcoholics Play*. New York: Ballantine Books.

Stevens-Long, J. (1992). *Adult Life*. Mt. View, CA.: Mayfield Publishing Co.

Stryker, S. and Statham, A. (1985). "Symbolic Interaction and Role Theory." Lindzey, G., and Aronson, E. (Eds.) *Handbook of Social Psychology*. Vol 1, Ed. Hillsdale, N.J.: Lawrence Erlbaum.

Tannen, D. (1992). *You Just Don't Understand*. New York: Ballantine Books.

Thompson, C. (1964). *On Women*. New York: New American Library.

Ulanov, A. (1971). *The Feminine In Jungian Psychology and in Christian Theology*. Evanston, Ill: Northwest University Press.

Ullman, J. (1986). *The Singles' Almanac*. New York: World Almanac Publications.

U.S. Dept. of Health and Human Services, Public Health Service. *Condoms and Sexually Transmitted Diseases...Especially AIDS*. FDA, Center for Devices and Radiological Health. HHS Publication FDA 90-4239.

U.S. Dept. of Labor, *Handbook of Labor Statistics*, 1989, 1990.

Vander, A.J., Sherman, J.H. and Luciano, D.S., (1975). *Human Physiology*. New York: McGraw-Hill Book Co.

Vanek, J. (1978). "Housewives as Workers." Voydanoff, Patricia (Ed.) (1984). *Work and Family: Changing Roles of Men and Women*. Palo Alto: Mayfield Publishing Co.

Vannoy-Hiller, D. and Philliber, W.W. (1989). *Equal Partners: Successful Women in Marriage*, Newbury Park: Sage.

Veroff, J., Douvan, E. and Kulka, R., (1981). *The Inner American*. New York: Basic Books.

Visher, E.B. and Visher, J.S. (1982). *Step-Families: Myths and Realities*. Secaucus, N.J.: Citadel Press.

Walker, K. and Woods, M. (1976). *Time Use: A Measure of Household Production of Goods and Services*. Washington, D.C.: American Home Economics Association.

Wallerstein, J. (1989). *Second Chances: Men, Women and Children a Decade After Divorce*. New York: Ticknor and Fields.

Watzlawick, P., Beavin, J.H. and Jackson, D.D. (1967). *Pragmatics of Human Communication*. New York: W.W. Norton.

Whelan, E.M. (1980). *A Baby, Maybe*. New York: Bobbs-Merrill Co, Inc.

White, M. and Epston, D. (1990). *Narrative Means to Therapeutic Ends*. New York: W.W. Norton.

Willi, J. (1982). *Couples in Collusion*. Claremont, CA: Hunter House.

Wilson, J. (1987). "Sexual Chemistry," *Ladies Home Journal*, Aug., 1987.

Woodman, M. (1982). *Addiction to Perfection*. Toronto: Inner City Books.

Young, M. and Willmott, P. (1973). *The Symmetrical Family*, New York: Pantheon.

Zibergeld, B. (1978). *Male Sexuality*. New York: Bantam Books.

Other New Harbinger Self-Help Titles

Call toll free, **1-800-748-6273,** to order books. Have your Visa or Mastercard number ready.

Or send a check for the titles you want to: **New Harbinger Publications, 5674 Shattuck Avenue, Oakland, CA 94609.** Include $2.00 for the first book and 50¢ for each additional book, to cover shipping and handling. (California residents please include appropriate sales tax.) Allow four to six weeks for delivery.

SINGLES RESOURCES
from Marin Publications

ORDER FORM

Please mail me the following items:

- ☐ Looking for Love in All the Right Places (audio tape)
- ☐ How to be Happily Single (audio tape)
- ☐ Romantic Charisma (audio tape)
- ☐ Initiating Contact & the Art of Flirting (audio tape)
- ☐ How to Select the Right Partner/Eliminating the Competition (audio tape)
- ☐ Self-Esteem for Singles (audio tape)
- ☐ How to Find a Lasting Relationship (240 page book)
- ☐ Singles Guide to the San Francisco Bay Area (208 page book)
- ☐ Singles Guide to Southern California (208 page book)
- ☐ A Good Man is Easy to Find in the San Francisco Bay Area (208 page book)
- ☐ A Good Man is Easy to Find in Southern California (216 page book)

$9.95 + $1.71 shipping & handling = **$11.66 per book or tape.**

Enclosed is my check for $		
Please charge my Visa or MC#		
Name:		Phone:
Address:		
City:	ST:	ZIP:

Mail to:

Marin Publications
4 Highland Ave.
San Rafael, CA 94901

Or order over the phone: (415) 459-3817.

Janet Z. Giler is a marriage and family therapist in private practice in West Los Angeles, counseling couples and singles. She has been in private practice since 1982, and has been a therapist for 20 years, working with behavioral medicine and biofeedback. She has been an adjunct Professor of Family Therapy at Pepperdine University in Los Angeles. She attended the University of California, Berkeley, and received her bachelor's degree in philosophy from the New School for Social Research in New York City. She received her master's degree in educational psychology from California State University, Northridge. She is currently a doctoral candidate at the Fielding Institute.

Janet Z. Giler is a member of the California Association of Marriage and Family Therapy and American Association of Marriage and Family Therapy. She is the author of *Archetype of the Wounded Healer: Study of an Urban Shaman*, and an article, "Infidelity in the 80s," which appeared in *Cosmopolitan* magazine in November, 1988, and author of two audiotapes, "How to Meet Men" and "Choosing the Right Mate."

photo by Richard Gatza

Kathleen Neumeyer has been a contributing editor of *Los Angeles* magazine since 1976, and is a freelance writer, with articles appearing in the *Ladies' Home Journal, New Woman, TV Time*, and the *Los Angeles Times Syndicate*. She is a member of the journalism faculty at California State University, Northridge, where she teaches advanced reporting and magazine article writing.

Kathleen Neumeyer is a graduate of the Medill School of Journalism at Northwestern University and is a member of the American Society of Journalists and Authors. She is a member of the Society of Professional Journalists, and a past president of the Los Angeles Chapter of the Society of Professional Journalists (1981). In 1983 she served as national chairperson of the Distinguished Service Awards of the Society of Professional Journalists. She has served five times as a judge in the Society of Professional Journalists Distinguished Service Awards. She is the author of hundreds of newspaper and magazine articles.